Rebuildir

of Agape Love

in 52 Days

Rebuilding the Wall

of Agape Love

in 52 Days

by

Sadie Bolton Sawyer

Rebuilding the Wall of Agape Love in 52 Days
Sadie Sawyer
AtL Publishing Co.
Copyright July 2018
ISBN- 978-1724502353

DEDICATION

I DEDICATE THIS DEVOTIONAL TO GOD our heavenly Father, Who so loved us that HE gave HIS only begotten SON. And to JESUS, Who is the ultimate gift of Agape Love for the redemption of our sin. And to HIS HOLY SPIRIT, Who sheds the Agape Love of God in our hearts.

Next, I dedicate this devotional in memory of my maternal grandmother, Sadie C. Williams; my paternal grandparents, Matthew and Leola Bolton; my loving parents, Wilmer and Daisy Bolton; my baby sister, Debra Emmitt; and to my in-laws, Melvin and Hazel Sawyer.

In addition, I thank GOD for the following persons that HE placed in my life to inspire and encourage me to write this devotional. First, I thank my beloved husband, Earnest Sawyer, who has demonstrated Agape Love for our 44 years of marriage; secondly, my loving daughters Christy Sawyer, Cabrina Smith, and Catina Batts; third, my beautiful, talented, and saved granddaughters, Isis Naomi Smith and Chloe Izabel Smith; and fourth, my handsome, talented and saved grandson Zion Jones, who always touches and agrees with me that Prayer Still Works. I want to acknowledge my Pastor, Reverend Conway Jones, and First Lady Debra Jones, who encouraged and urged me to complete this devotional in due season. I would further like to thank Pastor Jones, who I trusted because of his wisdom and knowledge of the Bible for accurate Scripture application.

Furthermore, I thank Pastor Lewis King who in 2004 prophesied my writing of this devotional. I also acknowledge Minister Marie Williams, who has been my midnight prayer partner for 18 years; Mrs. Alma Braxton and The Henrietta Brown's Prayer Warriors, along with Pastor Troy and The Secret Place Family, who all prayed for the completion of this devotional.

Finally, I thank Pastor Bobby Amezcua, my anointed graphic designer and my editor, Karolyn Jackson, who were both anointed and appointed by Him to bring about this devotional for His Honor and His Glory.

FOREWORD

Many are desperately searching for love in all the wrong places. For they do not understand that there are different kinds of love. There is man's love (eros and phileo) which is lacking in so many ways. And then there is a perfect and eternal love (agape love) that can only come from God Almighty, Maker of heaven and earth. In this little, but powerful book, the author shares an exciting love story; presented in a fifty-two-day devotional. These daily devotions reveal how much the Creator loves His Creation (all mankind); and longs to fill man's void for real love. Only God's agape love can completely satisfy man's need for love. And this book takes the reader into the profound depth of knowing God through His agape love; the unconditional love only a loving Father in heaven can provide. I pray that the message of this book be heard around the world; as a witness to a merciful, faithful, and kind heavenly Father; Whose love for man has no boundaries. For God so loved the world that He did the most He could do to provide a way for mankind to be reconciled to Him. He gave His only begotten Son, Jesus, to die on the Cross to forgive us of all our sin. What a magnificent Father, Who offers His love, the only real love that matters beyond this life. A love which keeps the faithful watching and waiting; to spend eternity with their Lord. Finally, as this book is read in faithful recognition of their loving heavenly Father; believers will remain in love with their first love—Jesus, their soon coming King. Maranatha! Come Lord Jesus, Come!!

Pamela Elaine Lockridge, MSW, Author
May 25, 2018

REVIEWS

Reading this devotional helps me keep God's agape love for me in perspective. This book has played a phenomenal part in keeping my priorities straight; as I utilize it to start each day meditating upon His unconditional love for me. As I learn about the deepness and profoundness of God's love, it gives me the strength I need; to rise above the fray in this dark and evil world. The glory of the Lord has risen upon me and I will spread His agape love to my family, friends and enemies; in a way that reflects the glory of my heavenly Father. Through this devotional God has revealed that, just as Nehemiah was distressed about the walls of the protection of God's love being breached (which left the condition of his homeland in ruin), believers must be as compassionate to see the hurting and broken lives of the lost restored, which is only possible by God's unfailing love. Nehemiah's mission is a metaphor for us today, to see that God wants His faithful to reconcile Him to all—individuals, couples, siblings, families, etc. I believe this devotional will open eyes about the ruins we see every day in the earth among mankind. Believers must pray, asking the Lord for the wisdom to put forth His plan of action. And rebuild the wall of agape love of God in 52 days that will span the earth; for the earth is the Lord's and all who dwell within.

Vi Jones, Evangelist
June 6, 2018

This devotional entitled, Rebuilding the Walls of Agape Love in 52 Days, is a result of God's Word coming to life. God's rhema Word is reflected by the willingness of this godly woman to obey the Spirit of the Living God, by taking the reader into the depths of the Father's love for mankind. I recommend this book because I personally know the author and she is truly described in Proverbs 31. She has received a call by her Lord to proclaim to the Body of Christ, that only unity through His agape love one to another; will fulfill the commission Christ gave His disciples. The commission of Christ to go and make disciples cannot be completed until believers commit to learning how to walk in His agape love. I can attest that this devotional has challenged me to be a disciple who comes to know the agape love of God, which I know is the only way I can fulfill the purpose on this earth He has called me to do for His Kingdom. As believers become infused with the fragrance of the holiness of the Lord by walking in His unconditional love among mankind, salvation will come to those who choose to know the Lord and be saved. This book definitely takes the reader to a place of intimate fellowship with the Father and His agape love. Furthermore, it takes the reader from glory to glory, and provides a level of courage and maturity in the Lord that opens up doors to more responsibility within the Kingdom of God. It leaves no doubt that the believer who walks in agape love will one day hear these words of the Lord: "Well done my good and faithful servant. . .enter into the joy of the Lord."

Pastor Conway T. Jones, Senior Pastor
Rock Island Church
June 4, 2018

This devotional is a powerful, life changing testament of God's agape love. God's agape love is embedded within the pages. These pages that reflect the agape love of God, are not dead parchment but alive with a restorative proclamation; that without God's amazing love, we are nothing. The Body of Christ must read this book, for it is a refreshing challenge to new and seasoned believers—who choose to continually walk in God's agape love. As I read it daily, it is causing me to desire a more vigilant pursuit and expression of love towards my heavenly Father and all of mankind. This devotional will help disciples of the Lord to rely on the simplicity and power of the Holy Scriptures to live out the great commission, which is becoming living expressions of God's love in the earth. This devotional presents God as approachable, available, supportive, forgiving, merciful, and compassionate; through His agape love. I wholeheartedly recommend this devotional to others because it is a precious rendition of the fullness and pure love that only our Creator can have for His creation. This devotional compels readers to look deep within for hidden hurt, unforgiveness, shame, and fear; and let God's unconditional love heal, restore, and take the place of anything that is not of Him. In addition, the devotional accurately instructs mankind to repent and turn from selfish ways, and turn to the only everlasting love that can transform the evil heart of mankind. The Father will make beauty from the ashes of a life lived in pride, if mankind will come to Him in humility; asking for His grace and mercy. Finally, this devotional reminds believers, that though not perfect, because of His faithfulness to forgive all sins, they are capable of being better representatives of Jesus Christ by abiding in His agape love.

Pastor Troy L. Campbell, Senior Pastor
The Secret Place Church
June 2, 2018

PREFACE

In September, 2008, while on a plane returning to Natchitoches, Louisiana from Washington, D.C., I began to meditate on an exhortation for our church's 52nd Annual. As I meditated on the number 52, my spirit revealed to me that Nehemiah and the Israelites rebuilt the wall of Jerusalem in fifty-two days. Immediately, I began to contemplate the question, "What exactly has the Rock Island Church congregation accomplished while serving the Lord Jesus Christ during its fifty-two years in existence?" For several days, I pondered this question. Finally, on October 5, 2008, I began to write a devotional entitled: Rebuilding the Wall of Agape Love in 52 Days. The devotional was completed in 2008 on November 25, by writing one devotional a day for 52 days. These daily devotions, based on the reflection of Nehemiah's relationship with the Lord, God's people, and the secular world, coincide and highlight particular events which are relevant today. This is highly significant and currently prophetic to the body of Christ by assisting Christians to overcome in an evil and secular society.

After completing my 52-day writing odyssey, I filed the daily devotionals journal away for almost eight years. For the first several years, it went inactive, as I neither read it nor made any changes to its content. Then, for the next four years, from time-to-time, I would access the journal to read it and, oftentimes, made updates to the original manuscript. I also solicited the help of others to read the journal for their opinions on its clarity or to proofread it for errors. During that time, I also researched and sought advice on how to get a manuscript published, but for the last seven years nothing happened until immediately after my mother's death in 2015. After this life-altering experience, I began to feel a sense of urgency to finish this devotional. So, at the behest of my granddaughters, Isis and Chloe, who promised that they would help me to stay on my timeline and to encourage my accountability for finishing this devotional, I began my journey of finishing a project that had been many years in the making.

The purpose of this devotional is to attempt to assist the reader in understanding the real meaning of agape love according to the Scripture in Nehemiah who was called by God to rebuild the wall in Jerusalem. The wall Nehemiah was called to build reflected God's mercy, grace, and protection from the enemies of Israel. In this devotional the agape love of God shown to Nehemiah is now fully accomplished through His Son Jesus, the Savior of the World. Nehemiah shows the intimate relationship God had with His people in the Old Testament; which foreshadowed Christ to come as Redeemer, to all those who would call upon His name for salvation today. This devotional is the revelation that God imparted to me, that shows the connection between the wall of the Old Testament (a fortress and refuge for God's people) then and now. The wall now represents the Agape Love that God has for His chosen people who have accepted His Son, who are now able, through the power of His Holy Spirit, to love all mankind as He does: unconditionally. I truly believe that those who are hungry for a closer and intimate walk with both the Lord and man—that reflects His agape love—will be assured an abundant blessing that only God Almighty can provide.

In 2016, I received an exhortation from two different clergy from the Secret Place Church in Bellflower, California. Elder William Boykins proclaimed that I should "stop running from my calling," which immediately motivated me to begin writing the devotional at this particular time of my life. The next encouraging message came from Pastor Troy Campbell telling me "do not despise small beginnings." Both of these prophetic declarations further confirmed that although I may have thought of this devotional as immaterial, it would be anything but insignificant. I now know through two witnesses that this book will not only fulfill God's will for my life of abundance in Him, but is extremely relevant for the church today. I praise God that even though this book may seem small, it has a powerful message.

In 2016, I printed a copy of the devotional for its critique and/or elaboration on its content. The word of the Lord came to Pastor Conway Jones of Rock Island Baptist Church saying "this was my season to finish this devotional" and that "I should not let this season pass." After receiving these dual prophesies, I immediately began to thank and praise God for the completion and publication of this devotional. I determined and set my goal to complete it in 2017.

In summation, I came to the point where loved ones and clergy began to emphatically encourage me to finish this million-dollar seller within a certain time period or deadline. As Pastor Campbell instructed me on the subject of "how to protect your increase when chaos increases", I understood this to mean that when the book begins to get into the hands of Christians, it will be an offensive weapon against God's defeated foe. Pastor's instructions made me realize that I must commit myself to specifically hide my increase from the enemy's power to steal it, by covering my increase with the blood of Jesus: even before it manifests!

My simple prayer has now become:

HELP ME HOLY SPIRIT!!!

INTRODUCTION

In this devotional, agape love is described, demonstrated, declared, decreed, and delivered. First, it is described in 1 Corinthians 13:4-8. "Love is patient and kind; love does not envy or boast; and is not arrogant or rude. It does not insist on its own way; it is not irritable or resentful; it does not rejoice at wrongdoing, but rejoices with the truth. Love bears all things, believes all things, hopes all things, endures all things. Love never fails. Next, it is demonstrated by God in John 3:16 – "For God so loved the world that He gave His only begotten Son to be crucified for the remission of our sins." It is demonstrated by Jesus' disciples in John 13:35 which states: "By this all men will know that you are my disciples because you have love one to another." Then, it is declared by Jesus when He proclaimed from the Cross in Luke 23:34, "Father, forgive them for they know not what they do." It was decreed by Jesus the first and great commandment in Matthew 22:37 which states: "Thou shalt love the Lord thy God with all thy heart, and with thy soul, and with all thy mind," and the second is like unto it, "Thou shalt love thy neighbor as thyself," as written in Matthew 22:39. Finally, it was delivered by the Holy Ghost in Romans 5:5b: "Because the love of God is shed abroad in our hearts by the Holy Ghost which is given unto us."

"For God so loved the world that He gave His only begotten Son, that whosoever believeth in Him shall not perish, but have everlasting life."

John 3:16

THAT'S AGAPE LOVE

True agape love was demonstrated by almighty, generous God

He gave His only begotten Son, Who shed His precious blood

And He chose to redeem us while we were still sinners.

Then because of God's grace, we are born again winners

Salvation empowers us to have love one to another

And our Savior's love, encourages us to convert our brother.

God's loves shed abroad by the Holy Spirit in our hearts;

Anoints us to walk the love walk by faith from the start

Phileo (brotherly love) cannot truly demonstrate agape love

Everlasting life and true love can only come from God above.

Love (agape) that is shown to family, enemies, and friends

Outlasts Eros (feeling-based romantic love)—a love that quickly ends

Verily I urge us through agape love, to make Jesus our Lord

Entering into His Presence, as we prepare to reap our reward.

FOUNDATIONAL SCRIPTURE

"So the wall was finished in the twenty and fifth day of the month E'lul, in fifty and two days."
Nehemiah 6:15

TODAY'S SCRIPTURE

"For God so loved the world, that he gave his only begotten Son, that whosoever believeth in him should not perish, but have everlasting life."
John 3:16

EXHORTATION: Love. You hear a lot about it, but do you really know what it means? "I want to know what love is, I know you can show me," is more than a popular song's lyrics. I praise my loving God for showing His agape love by giving His only begotten Son; Who shed His precious blood for the remission and forgiveness of sin. I thank God that we who have accepted His plan of salvation are covered by the blood of Jesus. He shows His agape love to all through His many acts of kindness to mankind. God demonstrates His love in every facet of our lives. He prepares a table before us in the presence of our enemies. He allows His sweet rain to fall down and wash both the just and the unjust alike. He encourages us to cast all our cares upon Him, for He cares for us. He never leaves us nor forsakes us. Lo, He will be with us until the end of time. He is our all and all. He loves us in spite of our shortcomings. It is by the amazing grace of the Lord God Almighty along with His selfless, sacrificial, unconditional agape love that leads man to repentance.

Who is love? "For God is love" (1 John 4:8b). How does He love us? "For God so loved the world, that he gave his only begotten Son, that whosoever believeth in him should not perish, but have everlasting life" (John 3:16). God's agape love required sacrificing His only begotten Son as a ransom for us—because we were born into a sin nature. He gave His only begotten Son, Jesus, to be our kinsman-redeemer. Jesus paid the price with His precious blood by becoming the sacrificial Lamb for our redemption. This is God's agape love being demonstrated for all to know and see that God really loves us. God's agape love is the greatest power on earth and provides believers with the strength and benefits they need to overcome in this dark and evil world. He is Jehovah-Jireh; our provider. He supplies all our needs according to His riches in glory by Christ Jesus. We know Him as a generous God who gives us our daily bread. We also know Him as a merciful and loving God. His mercies are new every morning.

PRAYER: Dear God, I present my body as a living sacrifice, holy and acceptable unto You, which is my reasonable service. God, I thank You for agape love that is being shed abroad in my heart. I thank You that I have the mind of Christ and a body that is fearfully and wonderfully made in Your image. God, I know in order to walk in unconditional agape love, I must be willing to sacrifice my money, my time, and my talents for all mankind. God, I need Your Holy Spirit to help me fulfill my God-ordained purpose of being a witness before sinners. Your Word says that through Your great and merciful plan of salvation, whosoever calls upon the name of Jesus, will be born again with the promise of eternal life with You; through Your great mercy and love for them. In Jesus' name, I pray. Amen.

THOUGHT: God's love requires sacrifice. Jesus sacrificed His life, so that I could have eternal life.

FOUNDATIONAL SCRIPTURE

"So, the wall was finished in the twenty and fifth day of the month E'lul,
in fifty and two days."
Nehemiah 6:15

TODAY'S SCRIPTURE

"As the Father hath loved me, so have I loved you;
continue ye in my love."
John 15:9

EXHORTATION: We often sing the little Vacation Bible School chorus: "Jesus loves me this I know, for the Bible tells me so. Yes, Jesus loves me. Yes, Jesus loves me. Yes, Jesus loves me. For the Bible tells me so." How do I know? Because, God so loved me, that He gave His only begotten Son, that whosoever believes in Him shall not perish, but have everlasting life. It is good to become a disciple or follower of Jesus. And it is very good to know that God loves me in spite of myself. In various situations in life, Satan, the enemy, tries to make us believe that God does not love us. So, instead of running to a loving God, we run toward Satan, who hates our very existence. A loving Jesus came so that we could have life and have it more abundantly. In contrast, Satan the hater, came to kill, steal and destroy.

Jesus commanded us to rebuild the wall in fifty-two days by abiding in His agape love. He showed His disciples how to continue to act and abide in His love. He wanted us to know that we must love each other just as He and the Father have love for each other, and the same love God has for us. How can I abide in His love in an unlovable situation? Jesus said, "If ye keep my commandments, ye shall abide in my love, even as I have kept my Father's commandments and abide in his love". Also, Jesus emphatically and lovingly exhorts, "This is my command, that ye love one another as I have loved you" (John 15:9-10,12). Today, let us begin to obey His commandments by having agape love for all mankind.

PRAYER: Father, God of love, let me continue to walk in love. I want to live a life of love. Help me love the unlovable. In Jesus' name, I choose today to walk in agape love with all mankind. I will love others as Jesus loves me. Thank You, Father, for Jesus. Father, when I am confronted with an unloving situation, let me remember to ask myself: "What would Jesus Do"? Thank You, Lord, for Your unconditional agape love that is shed abroad in my heart by the power of Your Holy Spirit. In Jesus' name, I pray. Amen.

THOUGHT: Agape love requires obedience. Trust and obey for there is no other way to be happy in Jesus but to trust and obey.

FOUNDATIONAL SCRIPTURE

"So, the wall was finished in the twenty and fifth day of the month E'lul,
in fifty and two days."
Nehemiah 6:15

TODAY'S SCRIPTURE

"Humble yourselves therefore under the mighty hand of God, that he
may exalt you in due time."
1 Peter 5:6

EXHORTATION: You may ask: (1) What does it mean to be humble? (2) How can I walk in agape love by humbling myself? (3) When am I to be humble? To be humble means to be devoid of pride and arrogance and to have a spirit of submission. Because I love God, I will submit by obeying His Word. I will esteem others better than myself. The Bible says, "Likewise, ye younger, submit yourselves unto the elder. Yea, all of you be subject one to another, and be clothed with humility: for God resisteth the proud, but giveth grace to the humble" (1 Peter 5:5).

Father, I thank You that I can humble myself under Your mighty hand. I pray, as Jabez prayed, that Your hand might be with me because all my times are in Your hand. Divine protection, love, joy, and peace have been granted to me today because I have divine favor with You and all mankind: "For this cause, I bow my knees unto the Father of Lord Jesus Christ. That Christ may dwell in my heart by faith; being rooted and grounded in His love" (Ephesians 3:14,17). And because of God's faithfulness and love for all mankind, we can humbly walk in agape love.

PRAYER: Father God, I bow down on my knees to You. I humbly submit to Your will. I know, Father God, that it is Your good pleasure to give me the kingdom. I daily submit my will to Your will. Because of Your agape love, Father God, I will love You as You love me. Your perfect love enables me, through Your Holy Spirit, to love all mankind; without hesitation or fear. I find myself drawn to Your authority over my life. It is because You are in ultimate control of my life, that I find my rest and peace in You. I wholeheartedly commit to walk in humility and love. In Jesus' holy name, I pray. Amen.

THOUGHT: God's love requires submission. I will say as Paul said, "Today I will bring my body {mind and spirit-emphasis} under subjection."

FOUNDATIONAL SCRIPTURE

*"So the wall was finished in the twenty and fifth day of the month E'lul,
in fifty and two days."*
Nehemiah 6:15

TODAY'S SCRIPTURE

*"Love the Lord, your God, with all your heart and with all your soul and
with all your mind and with all your strength."*
Mark 12:30

EXHORTATION: This first and great commandment is to, "Love the Lord, your God with all your heart and with all your soul and with all your mind and with all your strength" (Mark 12:30). "I really love the Lord; I really, really love the Lord. I love Him, I love Him—I really love the Lord" is one of my favorite choruses. I do love my Father in heaven more than I love anyone or anything else. I spend intimate fellowship time with my Father every day. It is because of this quiet time I spend alone seeking Him, that I grow in grace, mercy and love for others. I have peace knowing that He loves me; even when I am acting unlovable. I feel confident in my salvation through God's all-powerful and wonderful love for me, even though I still sin. I am emboldened to come before God's throne of grace to find help and mercy in time of need. What a friend I have in Jesus, Who sticks closer than a brother. When I fathom God's great love for me, how can I not respond by returning a sacrifice of love through worship and praise that is pleasing to Him? I dwell in His presence and draw near, instead of running away from Him when I stumble and sin. By spending time in His Word and in prayer, my faith rises. And it allows me to realize He loves me unconditionally and forever, no matter what comes my way to test me. He is pleased by my faith in Him. And I vow to keep my faith in Him until the end. I am also reminded, that when I worship Him I must do it in spirit and in truth; because this greatly pleases Him.

In order to be strengthened by agape love, we need to meditate daily on the Scripture in Mark 12:30. When we obey this command, it gives Him great joy. In Nehemiah 8:10, we read, "For the joy of the LORD is our strength". During our weakest moments, His strength is made perfect in our weakness. And God's perfect love will lift us up when we are at our lowest.

PRAYER: Lord, I want to love You with all my heart, with all my soul, with all my mind, and with all my strength. God, I will love You and others by denying myself and taking up the Cross and following You daily. I will seek Your will and yield my all to You. I will choose Jesus as Lord of all and as my personal Savior. I desire to walk in agape love daily. I choose to love, to forgive, and to treat others as I want to be treated. In Jesus' name, I pray. Amen.

THOUGHT: To show real love for our Father God, you must learn to worship Him in spirit and in truth.

FOUNDATIONAL SCRIPTURE

"So the wall was finished in the twenty and fifth day of the month E'lul,
in fifty and two days."
Nehemiah 6:15

TODAY'S SCRIPTURE

"And the second is like unto it, Thou shalt love thy neighbour as
thyself."
Matthew 22:39

EXHORTATION: Jesus said, "The first and great commandment is, "Thou shalt love the Lord thy God with all thy heart, and with all thy soul, and with all they strength, and with all thy mind." He continues, And the second is like unto it, "Thou shalt love thy neighbour as thyself". Further, He added, "On these two commandments hang all the laws and the prophets" (Matthew 22:37,39-40). I am grateful that His Word instructs me to obey the above commandments, so that I will be able to walk in agape love with all mankind. In times of peril when the threat of the enemy is trying to kill, steal, and destroy our entire beings with hate crimes on the local, the state, and the national level, it is good to know that I serve a loving God; Whose Holy Spirit empowers me to walk in His agape love.

Jesus says that if I truly love God and my neighbors, I will naturally keep His commandments. It would be a joy and a passion to love others as Jesus Christ, Who is the lover of our souls, loves us. Jesus encourages us not to think too highly of ourselves, but rather esteem others better than us. We must treat our neighbors the way we want to be treated. Therefore, we must endeavor to walk in agape love; by being a Good Samaritan to all mankind. We should always aspire to look beyond others' faults and see their needs. We all have great need of acceptance from one another in spite of our faults; for we were all sinners. And only through the God's amazing grace and tender mercies, is anyone able to be saved and walk in His agape love. We all stand equal at the foot of the Cross.

PRAYER: O Lord, have mercy on me. God, teach me how to always see others through Your loving eyes. I am resolved to love You; and my family and friends. Furthermore, I commit to love and pray for my enemies; as You give me the strength to do so. Father, I vow to always try to walk in agape love, by following Your example, by loving my neighbors as I love myself. In Jesus' name, I pray. Amen.

THOUGHT: Who are my neighbors? All of mankind from the least to the greatest.

FOUNDATIONAL SCRIPTURE

*"So the wall was finished in the twenty and fifth day of the month E'lul,
in fifty and two days."*
Nehemiah 6:15

TODAY'S SCRIPTURE

*"For God hath not given us a spirit of fear; but of power, and of love,
and of a sound mind."*
2 Timothy 1:7

*"There is no fear in love, but perfect love castest out fear: because fear
hath torment. He that feareth is not made perfect in love."*
1 John 4:18

EXHORTATION: "The fear of the Lord is the beginning of wisdom and knowledge, but fools despise wisdom and instructions" (Proverbs 1:7). The Word states, "If any of you lack wisdom, let him ask of God, that giveth to all men liberally, and upbraideth not, and it shall be given him" (James 1:5). Wisdom is the principal thing I seek, but in all my getting, I will get an understanding of God's unconditional agape love. In obtaining God's wisdom, I resign and remove myself from the acronym, FEAR, (i.e., False Evidence Appearing Real), because I have entrusted all my faith in my loving God. I believe my Father will enable me, through the unfailing power of His Holy Spirit, to walk daily in agape love; without any semblance in my life of false evidence appearing real.

God's Word says: "There is no fear in love, but perfect love casts out fear" (1 John 4:18a). I choose to love my heavenly Father and all mankind with agape love, which carries with it no fear. For the Word tells me that He has not given me a spirit of fear, but of power, love and a sound mind. God's agape love helps me to walk without fear in the valley of the shadow of death. And because I can totally trust in Him—I fear no evil—for my cup runs over with His agape love.

PRAYER: Dear Father God, thank You for protecting me against a spirit of fear by giving me a spirit of power and love and a sound mind. God, I will continue to lift my eyes to You, from which cometh my help. "Yea, though I walk through the valley of the shadow of death, I will fear no evil," because I know that my cup runneth over with agape love. I place my trust in Your Word that tells me that "perfect love casts out fear." Because I trust in Your Word, I have chosen to keep my mind on Your agape love. I will forever walk by faith and never by fear. In the name of Jesus, it is done. Amen.

THOUGHT: God says there is no fear in His perfect love. We must continually walk in faith and put our trust in a loving God.

FOUNDATIONAL SCRIPTURE

*"So the wall was finished in the twenty and fifth day of the month E'lul,
in fifty and two days."*
Nehemiah 6:15

TODAY'S SCRIPTURE

*"For, brethren, ye have been called unto liberty; only use not liberty for
an occasion to the flesh, but by love serve one another. For all the law
is fulfilled in one word, even in this; thou shalt love thy neighbour as
thyself."*
Galatians 5:13-14

EXHORTATION: To love thy neighbour as thyself, we must practice Paul's instructions: "This I say then, walk in the Spirit, and ye shall not fulfill the lust of the flesh." (Galatians 5:16). Also, desire to walk in the fruit of the Spirit, which is "love, joy, peace, longsuffering, gentleness, goodness, faith, meekness, and temperance; against such, there is no law" (vv. 22-23). Love is the fruit that we must possess to be able to walk in love, joy, peace, patience, goodness, kindness, faithfulness, gentleness and self-control. My desire is to be an agape love walker through God's grace and His mercy. While walking down agape love lane, I must remember to walk by faith and not by sight.

Paul commands believers to, "Through love, serve one another" (v. 13). Who can we serve today through the love of Christ, which has been shed abroad in our hearts by the Holy Spirit? Each day we can minister to everyone whose path we cross. As born-again Christians, we are empowered by the Holy Spirit to witness to our neighbors, our family, our friends, and even our enemies.; about what Christ has done for all mankind through His love. God will use us as laborers in His vineyard of souls. We will tell everyone about the agape love of God; as we walk along the path that God has ordained for us. There is no one from the least to the greatest, who does not need to understand His mercy and grace; which leads men to repent of their sins and come to Christ for salvation. His love draws mankind upon a grateful response to His agape love for them.

PRAYER: Father God, I thank You that You have commissioned us this day to serve one another through Your love. I will continue to walk in Your agape love. Father God, I choose to walk in agape love by walking in the fruit of the Spirit, which is love, joy, peace, patience, goodness, kindness, faithfulness, gentleness, and self-control. I surrender my flesh to You today, by denying myself and taking up the Cross and following Jesus daily. Because Jesus is love, I will grow stronger in love day by day. In Jesus' loving name, I pray. Amen.

THOUGHT: Because God showed His divine love for us by giving His only begotten Son to die for us, we should serve one another with the same sacrificial love He has for us.

FOUNDATIONAL SCRIPTURE

"So the wall was finished in the twenty and fifth day of the month E'lul, in fifty and two days."
Nehemiah 6:15

TODAY' SCRIPTURE

"Who shall separate us from the love of Christ? Shall tribulation, or distress, or persecution, or famine, or nakedness, or peril, or sword?"
Romans 8:35

EXHORTATION: I will let nothing separate me from the love of God. In these trying times, God's love is pivotal in my life. Every day I need God's love in every facet of my life and my being. Paul says, "For I am persuaded that neither death, nor life, nor angels, nor principalities, nor powers, nor things present, nor things to come, nor height, nor depth, nor any other creature, shall be able to separate us from the love of God, which is in Christ Jesus our Lord" (Romans 8:38-39). It is a joy to know that God will always have agape love for us. Even while we were sinners, He so loved us that He gave His only begotten Son to die on an old rugged Cross; so that we could receive eternal life living in His presence.

I humble myself under the mighty hand of God, knowing that, in due time, He will exalt me. I am determined, by the grace of God, to let nothing separate me from the love of God; which is in Christ Jesus our Lord. I can rest assured that I am forever loved by God, because now I know the truth of His love. And the truth of His agape love has set me free from sin and spiritual death. I thank the Lord that I will not be touched by the second death.

PRAYER: Father God, thank You for Your Holy Word that assures me that I need not let anything separate me from Your precious love. Your love guides my steps as I choose to walk in agape love. As Mary said, "Be it according to Your Word, God." Today, I boldly declare that I will let nothing separate me from the love of God; which is in Christ Jesus our Lord. In Jesus' name, I pray. Amen.

THOUGHT: Because of Jesus' great love and sacrifice, I will never be separated from God's love.

FOUNDATIONAL SCRIPTURE

"So the wall was finished in the twenty and fifth day of the month E'lul, in fifty and two days."
Nehemiah 6:15

TODAY'S SCRIPTURE

"A new commandment I give unto you, That ye love one another; as I have loved you, that ye also love one another. By this shall all men know that ye are my disciples, if ye have love one to another."
John 13:34-35

EXHORTATION: In these uncertain and tumultuous times, the world should be able to see that we are Christ's disciples because our lives reflect our Father in heaven by word and deed. The world will see our Father as we reveal Him by our love for the brethren; as well as our neighbors and our enemies.   God's agape love within me enables me to love Him with all my heart, with all my soul, with all my mind, and with all my strength. Also, it will make me love my neighbors as I love myself.   I know that by the aid of the Holy Spirit, I will be able to demonstrate agape love to my loved ones. Furthermore, I daily seek to be like my heavenly Father who said: "With love and kindness have I drawn them" (Jeremiah 31:3b). My desire is that all men will see that I am a disciple of Christ, because I have a genuine agape love for all mankind. I have fixed my heart to show God's agape love to a lost and dying world, by speaking words of encouragement and edification to everyone.

I was once challenged by a family member to be more Christ-like. "What do you see when you look in the mirror," he asked? I then began to ponder the following questions in my mind and applied them to my heart:

- Do I recognize the agape love of God that is at work in my life as a believer?
- Do I stop to consider if others are seeing the agape love of God at work in me?
- Do I demonstrate the agape love of God to all mankind; which includes my family, my friends, the lost, and my enemies?
- Do I show God's agape love in my walk, my talk, at work, when I play, while I'm driving, or even when I am at home all alone?

I realized these questions brought forth a powerful examination of my life. The Lord gave these questions to provide a comprehensive path to seeing myself as He sees me. My answers provide me with a view of myself from all angles. And floods my soul with His deep revelation of who I really am in Him. As I maintain a correct inventory of living my life through His agape love, all men will know that I am His beloved child.

PRAYER: Father God, I surrender all my life, plans, and dreams unto You. In the name of Jesus, I surrender any hatred, malice, strife and unforgiveness to You. I know that it is Your will and Your commandment that I should love others as Jesus loves me. The song lyrics say, "O How I Love Jesus, O How I Love Jesus, O How I Love Jesus because He first loved me." Father God, let all men know and see that I am Your disciple because I have love for all mankind, including my enemies. Let my every word be loving and kind as I keep my mind on You. I desire Your strength to love in word and deed, because Your Word commands me to be a doer of Your Word and not a hearer only. In Jesus' name, I pray. Amen.

THOUGHT: God, I will demonstrate Your agape love through many acts of compassion toward all mankind; especially those of the household of faith.

FOUNDATIONAL SCRIPTURE

"So the wall was finished in the twenty and fifth day of the month E'lul, in fifty and two days."
Nehemiah 6:15

TODAY'S SCRIPTURE

"And hope maketh not ashamed; because the love of God is shed abroad in our hearts by the Holy Ghost which is given unto us."
Romans 5:5

EXHORTATION: "How do I love thee? Let me count the ways." Sonnet 43 by Elizabeth Barrett Browning is an extremely popular adage. It provokes thoughts about the various ways that love can be shown from one to another. One way is through eros love which is a romantic type of love between a man and a woman. The other type of love is phileo love; which is a brotherly love between siblings, parents, friends, etc. Agape love is totally different and is not an earthly love that man can stir up. Agape love is Who God is. This love is only understood and received when an individual becomes born again by the Spirit of God. The Word of God tells about the depth and width of His love; which is unfathomable and incomprehensible to the minds of men—unless they are born again. Man cannot summon or create this kind of love. It is shed abroad in the heart of the believer by the power of His Holy Spirit. God's agape love is beyond the love that mankind can provide. God's love is supernatural; which is why man cannot comprehend its ability to transform a life of sin—into a life lived by faith that pleases Him. His Spirit that resides within the believers, enables them to walk in agape love with all mankind. Believers ask the Holy Spirit to help them to love as God loves. Believers learn to follow the teachings and the commandments of Jesus and His Father to walk in agape love. Believers are exhorted to follow the examples of Jesus and His Father, Who are both our examples when it comes to demonstrating agape love. Believers who walk in His love, can receive no accolades for it. They must give all the glory and praise to Him. They must maintain humility and thankful hearts for what only He can do within them. He softens the believers' hearts, as they choose not to no longer live and walk with those who live in darkness.

Paul boldly states, "But God commendeth His love toward us, in that, while we were yet sinners, Christ died for us", (Romans 5:8, KJV, emphasis added). Also, John declares, "For God so loved the world that he gave his only begotten Son, that whoever believeth in him shall not perish, but have everlasting life" (John 3:16). Jesus brought His supernatural love to a dark and lost world. Every person is provided the opportunity to be saved; through the sacrificial Lamb of God Who died on the Cross for our sins. Accept Jesus into your heart now, if you do not know Him, for He is the Savior of the World. Ask Him to make Himself real to you and He promises He will. He said that whosoever would call upon Him—shall be saved!

This exhortation makes me glad that I have decided to walk in God's agape love. I will lovingly shout it from the housetop that God is love. I am so thankful His love has set me free to proclaim to the world His ultimate plan of salvation.

PRAYER: Father God, give me Your love that changes hearts and minds. Receive my gratefulness for Your Holy Spirit in my life; that increases my capacity to love beyond man's limited means of loving another. Please continually keep my heart filled with Your all-encompassing agape love for mankind. Help me every day to show that I am one of Your disciples; as I walk in Your amazing love. In Jesus' loving name, I pray. Amen.

THOUGHT: God's agape love is shed abroad in our hearts, by the power of God; for the purpose of completing the good work that He started in His children. His work in us is to bring us to perfect, mature, and holy people.

FOUNDATIONAL SCRIPTURE

*"So the wall was finished in the twenty and fifth day of the month E'lul,
in fifty and two days."*
Nehemiah 6:15

TODAY'S SCRIPTURE

*"And we have known and believed the love that God hath to us. God is
love; and he that dwelleth in love dwelleth in God, and God in him."*
1 John 4:16

EXHORTATION: I know what I know, and I believe what I believe. I
know and believe that God is love and, because I dwell in God's agape
love, I dwell in God. And He dwells in me. This promise is for ALL
who dwell in God. How can I know that I am dwelling in God's agape
love? Jesus instructs us in this verse, "Abide in me, and I in you. As the
branch cannot bear fruit by itself, unless it abides in the vine, neither
can you, unless you abide in me" (John 15:4). Also, He states, "If ye
keep my commandments, ye shall abide in my love, even as I have kept
my Father's commandments, and abide in his love" (v. 19). I praise my
Father in heaven for His comfort and assurance that I will abide in His
loving presence for all eternity.

I am so thankful for eternal salvation through the blood of Jesus that paid
the full price to reconcile me back to my Father in heaven. Your Word
tells me, "And ye shall know the truth and the truth shall make you free"
(John 8:32). Freedom is costly. It costs the life of the precious Son of
God, Jesus, to save me from my sin. Therefore, I cannot boast, I can only
bow low before my King; Who paid a high price for me to be able to
become a child of the Most High God.

PRAYER: Heavenly Father, I come boldly before Your throne of grace; as I am drawn by Your agape love. I am so thankful that Your love dwells in me. As I surrender to Your almighty power which will give me all the strength I need to be loving and kind to all mankind. Your Word says, "The LORD hath appeared of old unto me. Saying, yea, I have loved thee with an everlasting love, therefore, with lovingkindness have I drawn thee". God, I praise You that through Your Holy Spirit, I can walk in Your agape love all the days of my life. Lord, I thank You for drawing me with Your lovingkindness. In Jesus' name, I pray. Amen.

THOUGHT: I wholeheartedly believe that God's agape love dwells in me.

FOUNDATIONAL SCRIPTURE

*"So the wall was finished in the twenty and fifth day of the month E'lul,
in fifty and two days."*
Nehemiah 6:15

TODAY'S SCRIPTURE

*"Though I speak with the tongues of men and of angels, and have not
charity (love), I am become as a sounding brass or a tinkling cymbal."*
I Corinthians 13:1

EXHORTATION: What is that sound? Is it the sound of agape love or is it simply a lot of nothing? What does love have to do with anything? Love has everything to do with everything. Why? Because God is love! It would be so phenomenal if all the sounds that are coming over the airways could exude an abundance of agape love. However, it is extremely heartbreaking and tragic, that rather than love, the majority of sounds that are being broadcast over the airways are ominous sounds. Cruel sounds of hostility, anger, ill-will, resentment, apathy, contempt, antagonism which radiate contempt among unbelievers. The Word states, "My little children, let us not love in word, neither in tongue; but in deed and in truth" (1 John 3:18). The Almighty God is simply saying, "My little children do not become as a sounding brass or a tinkling cymbal {as the world-emphasis}; but a sweet sound that proclaims My agape love to the world".

Because we are God's children, He wants us to demonstrate agape love in both deed and in truth. We talk about how much we love each other, but oft times we fail to walk in the Spirit; showing His grace and mercy. We say, "I love you," but what happens when others despitefully use us. Our first line of response is usually to retaliate in kind. We should, however, take care to assure that we respond as Jesus responded while hanging on the old rugged Cross: "Father, forgive them, for they know not what they do" (Luke 23:34a).

PRAYER: Father, I want to speak the language of Your love with a powerful and encouraging voice; so that my life becomes more than a sounding brass or a tinkling cymbal. I want to make a joyful noise, filled with the representation of Your agape love. Lord, help me demonstrate Your agape love. And help me show all mankind Your grace and mercy through gracious deeds; as I follow the Lamb. Father God, I know that love is compassion in action. I know that actions speak louder than words. Therefore, I implore Your gracious strength to demonstrate to all men, that I am a doer of the Word and not a hearer only. In Your strength and power that enables me to love like you, I vow to love those I would not normally choose to love. Furthermore, I vow to forgive those I do not believe deserve it. Dear Lord, keep me in Your love that surpasses all understanding. In Jesus' name, I pray. Amen.

THOUGHT: I will not only speak of God's agape love, I will demonstrate it by loving and treating others the way I want to be treated.

FOUNDATIONAL SCRIPTURE

"So the wall was finished in the twenty and fifth day of the month E'lul,
in fifty and two days."
Nehemiah 6:15

TODAY'S SCRIPTURE

"And though I have the gift of prophecy, and understand all mysteries,
and all knowledge; and though I have all faith, so that I could remove
mountains, and have not charity (love), I am nothing."
I Corinthians 13:2

EXHORTATION: What does love have to do with it? Love has everything to do with it! If I do not have love, I have nothing. A heart filled with agape love will edify my gift of prophecy. It will increase my understanding of all mysteries and all knowledge. When I walk in love by trusting that He alone knows what is best for me, this kind of faith pleases my Father in heaven. As I walk in His love, there is nothing good that my loving Father withholds from me. And as my sole provider, He provides everything for me that pertains to life and godliness. If I do not have something I desire, it is not because God is being unloving or unkind. I do not have things I pray for at times because God knows best what I need. As I draw near to Him and He draws near to me, I pray more in line with His will for my life. And the more I surrender to Him, the more I begin to understand and receive His guidance towards the plan and purpose He has for me to live out on this earth. God's agape love has everything to do with everything, because to know Him is to know real love.

As I meditate on today's Scripture, I give God all the glory and the praise for His agape love. His unfailing love has tremendous provision for me that is undeniable. I am now accepted in the beloved; which provides that I am a joint heir with Jesus Christ, a member of the Body of Christ, and a member of Your royal priesthood. And as I walk this foreign land, knowing these truths empower me to be a bold witness for Your Son. How can I continue to proclaim this stupendous declaration to a dying world that desperately need the Savior, Jesus Christ? By continuing to ask the Holy Spirit to make the love of my Father a reality in my life. And because of Your great love, I have no fear of what the world can do to me. I can boldly declare that I am an overcomer by the blood of the Lamb and the word of my testimony. And because of this, I have been given entrance into eternal life with You.

PRAYER: Gracious God, let me continue to walk in Your agape love so that my gift of prophecy, my understanding of all mysteries and knowledge, and my mountain-moving faith will not be in vain. Thank You Father, that Your agape love reigns supreme within my heart. Your love brings me to my knees and helps me accomplish Your will in my life as I am strengthened by Christ. I am so grateful that Your Holy Spirit helps me to be all that I can be. In the powerful name of Jesus, I pray. Amen.

THOUGHT: Without God's agape love, I am nothing.

FOUNDATIONAL SCRIPTURE

"So the wall was finished in the twenty and fifth day of the month E'lul,
in fifty and two days."
Nehemiah 6:15

TODAY'S SCRIPTURE

"And though I bestow all my goods to feed the poor, and though I give
my body to be burned, and have not charity
(love) it profiteth me nothing."

I Corinthians 13:3

EXHORTATION: Do you want to remain in position to receive the reward that only your heavenly Father can give you? Then give as God has given to you, in agape love. Paul explains the following method of giving to the Corinthians: "Every man according as he purposeth in his heart, so let him give; not grudgingly, or of necessity: for God loveth a cheerful giver" (2 Corinthians 9:7). Some men may think that, in their hearts, they will begrudgingly give all their goods to feed the poor, because this is what God requires of them. Jesus said to the rich young ruler, "If thou wilt be perfect, go and sell all that thou hast, and give to the poor, and thou shalt have treasure in heaven; and come and follow me" (Matthew 19:21). Some of us are just like the ruler, especially when it comes to giving of our profits/treasure we have laid up on this earth. We fail to realize that everything we have comes from the Lord above. God calls us to walk in His agape love, so we realize that because of His love we have what we have anyway. And because of His love for us, we can give freely of our time, money, or whatever we have that others may need more than we do. We then acquire the ability to believe and trust that our loving Father has no problem meeting our needs and desires; as we imitate His giving heart towards our fellow man. But when man chooses to think of himself as the ruler over all he has, he is filled with sorrow and lack. When man would rather keep the pseudo-love for the things of this world, instead of sharing God's agape love with all mankind, he is at ill will (enmity) with God.

Some may think that if they give their bodies to be burned, this would be a well-pleasing sacrifice unto God. But Paul says, "I beseech you therefore, brethren, by the mercies of God, that ye present your bodies a living sacrifice, holy, acceptable unto God, which is your reasonable service" (Romans 12:2). Let us choose to obey God's commandments of agape love, by choosing to live a life of love in our mortal bodies through the Holy Spirit that dwells in us. Let us be ready to give of God's provision to those in need (whatever that may be), when God moves our hearts to do so.

PRAYER: Father God, teach me to love as You love—not merely to be seen or accepted by men. Help me know how to please You with my acts of giving. Let me live my life for others' interests and not just my own, as You have commanded. Because You love a cheerful giver, let me always give cheerfully whatever You ask me to give. Father God, I know that the safest place to be is in Your will. I know Your will is that I give to others for their needs as well as for the furtherance of Your kingdom—with a grateful heart for what You have given me. I pray for the passion to give from a heart free of resentment, because of Your agape love for me. In Jesus' name, I pray. Amen.

THOUGHT: Any act of kindness or sacrifice profits us nothing if we don't do them in agape love.

FOUNDATIONAL SCRIPTURE

"So the wall was finished in the twenty and fifth day of the month E'lul, in fifty and two days."
Nehemiah 6:15

TODAY'S SCRIPTURE

"Charity (love) suffereth long, and is kind; charity (love) envieth not; charity (love) vaunteth not itself, is not puffed up."
1 Corinthians 13:4

EXHORTATION: How much do I love you? I want to love you as Christ loved us, when He laid down His life for our sins. I would like to emphasize that Jesus is the Light of the world. I want the love of God that is being shed in my heart, to radiate to all mankind—who are trapped in a dark cold world of hatred.

1 Corinthians 13:4 gives us three descriptions of agape love.

Love is longsuffering and is kind. Two of the fruit of the Spirit are patience and kindness. Longsuffering is defined as having long-lasting patient endurance during an offense. Kindness is described as the quality of being generous and considerate. Agape love combines these two qualities when an offense comes our way. These two godly qualities make us act with His compassion during unpleasant situations believers face from anyone: believers or unbelievers.

Love envies not. Love is not jealous nor does it show resentment toward others. It is not aroused by another's advantage or their possession. Paul

49

admonishes us, "Therefore encourage one another and build one another up, just as You are doing" (1 Thessalonians 5:11, ESV). Elizabeth O'Connor, a noted famous author, wrote that, "Envy is a symptom of a lack of appreciation of our own uniqueness and self-worth. Each of us has something to give that no one else does." If each of us indeed has something to give, it becomes apparent that envy is a monumental waste of time. Walking in God's agape love has the ability to invalidate envy in every offensive situation we may face. We must be encouraged to make better use of our time; by walking in love instead of jealousy or envy towards others.

Love vaunteth not itself—it is not puffed up. Love does not boast, and it is not proud. Those that humble themselves under the mighty hand of God are truly walking in agape love. Also, Paul states, "Do nothing from rivalry or conceit, but in humility count others more significant than yourself" (Philippians 2:3, ESV).

PRAYER: God, I want to walk daily in the humility of agape love. Help me through Your Holy Spirit that lives within not to be boastful, nor too proud to do Your will. God, I will not envy or covet. In the name of Jesus, I surrender to Your will. I will show Your love through kindness and longsuffering. In the name of Jesus, I pray. Amen.

THOUGHT: Agape love is patient and kind. It shows no malice and is not prideful.

FOUNDATIONAL SCRIPTURE

"So the wall was finished in the twenty and fifth day of the month E'lul, in fifty and two days."
Nehemiah 6:15

TODAY'S SCRIPTURE

(Love) "Doth not behave itself unseemly, seeketh not her own, is not easily provoked, thinketh no evil."
1 Corinthians 13:5

EXHORTATION: A secular songwriter wrote and recorded the song entitled, Love Will Make You Do Wrong. In stark contrast, according to the Bible, "Love will make you do that which is right in God's Holy sight." God's Word tells of His agape love which is powerful and all-sufficient. And this unconditional love "does not behave itself unseemly" (1 Corinthians 13:5a). In other words, love is not rude, easily provoked, or entertains evil thoughts. Paul declares: "Love seeks not her own" (v. 5b). Paul further instructs us to "esteem others better than ourselves" (Philippians 2:3b). Paul goes on to describes how believers are to treat their brethren, "And we beseech you, brethren, to know them which labour among you, and are over you in the Lord, and admonish you; And to esteem them very highly in love for their work's sake. And be at peace among yourselves (1 Thessalonians 5:12-13).

Love is not easily provoked, but seeks to be at peace with all mankind. James instructs, "Wherefore, my beloved brethren, let every man be swift to hear, slow to speak, slow to wrath" (James 1:19). These actions describe how love is manifested when it thinks no evil and brings forth good in the sight of all men" (Romans 12:17b). Therefore I will, "Be not overcome of evil, but overcome evil with good" (v. 21). I choose to not allow evil to have control over me through my senses or speech. I vow to see no evil, speak no evil, nor listen to evil. Through Jesus, God's gift of agape love, I will strive to see, speak, and hear only what is good, for God is good. God's Word is the plumb line and power by which I vow to live a holy life before Him.

PRAYER: Father God, Your unfailing love causes me to be made righteous by Christ Jesus. Because I desire to live in right standing with You, I seek first Your kingdom and Your righteousness and all things will be added to me. I seek to be kind instead of rude. I seek not my own, but what is best for others. I will not be easily provoked because I walk in agape love, which is powerful to keep me at rest in You, through a sound and calm mind. I will not think evil because I have the mind of Christ; which causes me to dwell on Your truth. And as I follow the Lamb, surely goodness and mercy shall follow me all the days of my life. Thank You, Father God. In Jesus' name, I pray. Amen.

THOUGHT: As a man thinks, so is he. Therefore, I choose to think on things that are praiseworthy, such as God's amazing agape love.

FOUNDATIONAL SCRIPTURE

"So the wall was finished in the twenty and fifth day of the month E'lul, in fifty and two days."
Nehemiah 6:15

TODAY'S SCRIPTURE

(Love) "Rejoiceth not in iniquity, but rejoiceth in the truth."

I Corinthians 13:6

EXHORTATION: 1 Corinthians 13:6 teaches that, "Love does not delight in evil, but rejoices with the truth." The questions then become: (1) Who should rejoice? (2) When should they rejoice? (2) How should they rejoice? (4) Why should they rejoice?

Because God so loved the world that He gave His only begotten Son as a ransom for our sins so that we are saved, and we can have eternal life. Who should rejoice? Luke emphasizes that, "Believers rejoice because their names are written in the Lamb's book of life" (Luke 10:20b). When should believers rejoice? Jesus said, "Blessed are you when men hate you, when they exclude you, and insult you and reject your name as evil because of the Son of man. Rejoice in that day and leap for joy" (vv. 22-23). I choose to continually rejoice in the Lord no matter the circumstances of life. And this is only possible when I ponder His unfathomable love.

How do believers rejoice? Rejoicing is an outward expression through praise and worship towards a loving Father. Rejoicing as the Lord encourages us to do comes from a heart filled with joy expressed through the singing of hymns and spiritual songs. Rejoicing is also seen as believers adore

God by bowing, kneeling, or raising of hands to the One Who sits on the Throne in heaven. Why believers rejoice? Believers rejoice because of the truth about God's agape love for all mankind. God's agape love does not compel us to rejoice in iniquity, but to rejoice in our salvation, for great is our reward in heaven. I am overjoyed because this is the day that the Lord has made, and I will rejoice and be glad in it, because I am actively rebuilding the wall when I willfully choose to walk in agape love.

PRAYER: Father God, Your Word says, "To rejoice with those who rejoice and to weep with those who weep". And because I love my neighbors as myself, I will let Your wonderful love that dwells in my heart, be extended to my neighbors; so all men will know that I am Your child. I will not rejoice when anyone, including my enemy, falls into iniquity. Instead, I will seek to restore and reconcile all mankind back to You as I show forth Your agape love to them. Lord, You said in Your Word, "With lovingkindness have I drawn thee". I go forth as Your love draws me to surrender my life and will to You. In Jesus' name, I pray. Amen.

THOUGHT: The love and truth of a loving God always cause us to rejoice.

FOUNDATIONAL SCRIPTURE

"So the wall was finished in the twenty and fifth day of the month E'lul, in fifty and two days."
Nehemiah 6:15

TODAY'S SCRIPTURE

(Love) "Beareth all things, believeth all things, hopeth all things, endureth all things."

1 Corinthians 13:7

EXHORTATION: The greatest gift that anyone can have is the gift of unconditional agape love. The songwriter wrote:

Love lifted me!
Love lifted me!
When nothing else could help,
Love lifted me.

I thank God that my spirit is lifted daily because of His agape love. His love makes me want to lovingly encourage others to love as He loves. I am inspired by the Holy Spirit to edify and build up those who are broken-hearted and burdened by the trials of this life. Despite my sin, His love enables me to know that Jesus loved and died for me. Because Jesus bore my sin on the Cross, I can help bear the burdens of those who have fallen—by extending to them what He offered me: His plan of salvation by His grace, His mercy, and His agape love.

God is love. This means He can do nothing that is not loving. It also means He always protects and bears all things. Therefore, I can always trust and believe all things He does are for my good. The psalmist declares, "The LORD delights in those who fear Him, who put their hope in His unfailing love" (Psalm 147:11). That 'hope' comes from knowing that He can do nothing except love me, because I am His child. Paul said, "May the Lord direct your hearts into God's love and Christ's perseverance" (1 Thessalonians 3:5, NIV). This, God's Word, tells me that His love endures forever.

PRAYER: Father God, Your Word causes me to believe, to hope, to endure, and to trust all things that You are to me. Because of Your agape love, I can trust that You will never leave me nor forsake me. You show Your faithfulness through Your Word of love to me every day. Your loving arms are strong enough for me to lean upon and find protection. Your love leads me to: bear all things, believe all things, hope all things, endure all things. And Your magnificent love will never end, but last throughout all eternity. And I will dwell in the house of the Lord forever and ever. In Jesus' name, I pray. Amen.

THOUGHT: God's love is unconditional and everlasting. His agape love reigns supreme in every situation.

FOUNDATIONAL SCRIPTURE

*"So the wall was finished in the twenty and fifth day of the month E'lul,
in fifty and two days."*
Nehemiah 6:15

TODAY'S SCRIPTURE

*"Charity (love) never faileth. And now abideth faith, hope, charity,
(love) these three; but the greatest of these is charity (love)."*
1 Corinthians 13:8a, 13

EXHORTATION: The Word assures us that, "Charity (love) never faileth" (1 Corinthians 13:8a). We know this to be true because God is love and God cannot fail. We can, therefore, have ultimate confidence in His unfailing agape love. I know that I can lean on and depend on this powerful promise because God's Word will remain forever. Heaven and earth will pass away, but God's Word will never pass away.

Faith in God is reliance, loyalty, and complete trust in Him alone. Because Jesus is the author and the finisher of our faith, we can be assured that we can walk in agape love with all mankind. And with this knowledge, love and faithfulness should be our daily companions. King Solomon stated: "Let love and faithfulness never leave you; bind them around your neck, write them on the tablet of your heart" (Proverbs 3:3, KJV, paraphrased).

Hope is to desire something with confident expectations of its fulfillment. Paul proclaims that, "Faith is confidence in what we hope for and assurance about what we do not see" (Hebrews 11:1, NIV). 1 Corinthians 13:13 reveals that, "Love is the greatest of all human qualities and is the very essence of Who God is." John teaches, "Whoever does not love, does not know God; because God is love" (1 John 4:8). Love involves unselfish service to others and, to show it, gives evidence that you care. Faith culminates in the purposeful acts of agape love believers portray; because Christ lives within them. That God's disciples walk in love, is the foundation and content of God's requirements from His people. And the believers' hope in Christ, creates the attitude and focus that motivates them to love others as well as themselves. When faith and hope align in the lives of the believers who are finally freed from sin to love completely, they subsequently come to love as God loves.

PRAYER: Father God, I thank You for giving me a measure of faith. I know that without faith, it is impossible to please You. Your Word says that faith is the substance of things hoped for and the evidence of things not seen. This gives me hope that I can become perfect as You are perfect; because I know that the same Spirit that raised Christ from the dead dwells within me. The knowledge of Christ's presence within me, increases my faith and hope that I will be able to do Your will in my life. I am so very thankful that because Christ lives in me, I will walk in Your unfailing agape love forever. In Jesus' name, I pray. Amen.

THOUGHT: God's greatest attribute is His unfailing agape love. God is Love!

FOUNDATIONAL SCRIPTURE

"So the wall was finished in the twenty and fifth day of the month E'lul, in fifty and two days."
Nehemiah 6:15

TODAY'S SCRIPTURE

"To everything there is a season, and a time to every purpose under the heaven. A time to love."
Ecclesiastes 3:1, 8a

EXHORTATION: "What the world needs now is love sweet love, it's the only thing that there's just too little of." These lyrics of a popular songwriter should be resounding throughout the world. The 21st century with all its novelty has not been able to diminish hate throughout the world. Men's hearts have waxed cold because they are looking at what is going on in the world through human eyes. The natural appearance of mankind's actions in the world is full of hate. But there is a remnant of God in the world, who love Jesus with all of their hearts. Love still exists because of Christians who serve a loving God Who not only commands His children to love mankind as He does, but enables them through His Spirit to love them. This is the good news that all mankind needs to hear; the Gospel of Jesus Christ.

What time is it? It is time for us to love each other as God loves us. God demonstrated His agape love to us while we were yet sinners. He gave His only begotten Son, Jesus, to be crucified for our sins. HALLELULAH, THAT'S AGAPE LOVE! It is now time that we, as followers of Christ, begin to demonstrate that same agape love for each other and the people, tribes, and nations of the world.

The Christmas season includes this popular phrase from a Christmas carol, "Tis the Season to be Jolly". However, for each of us, every day should bring with it the selfless motto, "Tis the season to be loving". Solomon teaches that, "A friend loveth at all times" (Proverbs 17:17a). He further explains that, "God has made everything beautiful in its time" (Ecclesiastes. 3:11a). It is a beautiful and relevant time for showing God's love to the lost and dying world.

PRAYER: Heavenly Father, thank You that I am alive for such a time as this. Thank You for this season and this time that I am being empowered to walk daily in Your agape love. You said in Your Word that, "There is a time to love." I know that it is high time that I love You, Father God, with all my heart, with all my soul, with all my mind, and with all my strength. I know that it is also time that I love my neighbors as I love myself. I will always love, because I know that, "what the world needs now is Your love, sweet love." In Jesus' loving name, I pray. Amen.

THOUGHT: This is the season and the time to walk in agape love.

21

FOUNDATIONAL SCRIPTURE

*"So the wall was finished in the twenty and fifth day of the month E'lul,
in fifty and two days."*
Nehemiah 6:15

TODAY'S SCRIPTURE

*"Greater love hath no man this, that a man lay down his life
for his friends."*

John 15:13

EXHORTATION: Jesus states, "My command is this, Love each other as I have loved you" (John 15:12). Then He states, "I call you friends because you keep my commandments" (v. 14). Also, Jesus said, "Greater love hath no man than this, that a man lay down his life for his friends" (v. 13). Jesus explains, "No man took my life, I laid it down" (John 10:18). Our almighty and loving God so loved the world, that He asked His Son to become our sacrifice and pay the ransom for us while we were yet sinners. I thank Jesus for choosing to take up the Cross and die upon it as the spotless Lamb of God, that took away the sin of the world.

We should always praise God for His grace, His mercy, His goodness, and His agape love—a love so great that, when we receive Jesus as our personal Savior, we also receive the benefits of salvation, justification, sanctification, and redemption through the blood of the Lamb.

Jesus is the sacrificial Lamb. He was led as a sheep to the slaughter and, because we are His friends, He never said a mumbling word. He simply gave up the ghost for His friends. Jesus is a friend that sticks closer than a brother. He offers us unconditional agape love, instead of brotherly (phileo) love. He loves us in spite of our shortcomings.

PRAYER: Father God, thank You that we have an awesome friend in Jesus. He is a friend in whom we can put our total trust. I thank You, God, that Jesus will never leave us nor forsake us. He is a friend that sticks closer than a brother. Jesus said, "You have not chosen me, but I have chosen you". Thank You, Father God, that Jesus showed us how much He loved us by laying down His life for us. What a friend we have in Jesus, but not only a friend, we are joint heirs with Him. To show the love of Jesus, we must let our light shine so that men will see our good works and glorify the Father as we walk in agape love. In Jesus' name, I pray. Amen.

THOUGHT: Jesus demonstrated His great love when He laid down His life for all mankind, whom He richly desires to one day become His friends. He wishes that no man perish, but that all would come to Him and be saved.

FOUNDATIONAL SCRIPTURE

"So the wall was finished in the twenty and fifth day of the month E'lul,
in fifty and two days."
Nehemiah 6:15

TODAY'S SCRIPTURE

"We love him, because he first loved us."

1 John 4:19

EXHORTATION: "I really love the Lord. I really love the Lord. You don't know what He's done for me. He gave me the victory," is a familiar chorus that we sang at our local church during Circular Prayer Time. Many times, we sing the chorus, religiously, over and over. However, God wants us to worship Him in spirit and in truth. We shall know the truth and the truth shall make us free. I know that these words are true: "I love God because He first loved me." I am paraphrasing the following verses: "Love and you shall be loved, good measure, pressed down and shaken together, and running over shall men love us" (Luke 6:38), as Christ also loves the church" (Ephesians 5:25).

John asks, "If a man says I love God, and hateth his brother who he hath seen, how can he love God whom he hath not seen" (1 John 4:20)? God wants us to demonstrate His agape love by showing love one to another. Jesus said that this example of love one to another is how all men will know that we are His disciples. I will love God with all my heart, with all my soul, with all my mind, and with all my strength. I will also love my neighbors and my enemies as the Lord commands. I will then be able to love myself in a selfless manner, without becoming conceited or prideful. To love our enemies is a foreign and seemingly impossible request, until we see the example of our Lord Jesus on the Cross in our place. Christ showed us that love is more than emotion, it is a choice and commitment to always act in a loving manner on behalf of others, even for those who are undeserving of it. Jesus taught and demonstrated His different kind of love; in all His relationships with His friends and foes.

Most of the time we, as Christ's followers, want to show love to each other in:

Eros   - Romantic love between a man and a woman

Phileo - Brotherly love between siblings, parents, extended family and friends

PRAYER: Father God, I want to love You, not only because You first loved me, but because You command me to love You with all my heart, with all my soul, with all my mind, and with all my strength. God, I am walking in agape love with my brethren, whom I see every day because, if I hate them, I become a liar when I say that I love You, whom I have not seen. Thank You, Father God, for allowing me to walk in agape love with You and with all mankind. In Jesus' name, I pray. Amen.

THOUGHT: We should strive to show agape love to all mankind, for it will be returned to us a hundredfold—by Jesus—Who first loved us and gave Himself a living sacrifice.

FOUNDATIONAL SCRIPTURE

"So the wall was finished in the twenty and fifth day of the month E'lul, in fifty and two days."
Nehemiah 6:15

TODAY'S SCRIPTURE

"But the end of all things is at hand; be ye therefore sober, and watch unto prayer. And above all things have fervent charity (love) among yourselves, for charity (love) shall cover a multitude of sins."
1 Peter 4:7-8

EXHORTATION: In the cross-reference of the above KJV Verse 7 with NIV Verse 7, John is referencing the last days between Christ's first and second comings (See 1 John 2:18). Since no man knows neither the hour nor the second when the Son of God, Jesus will return, it is expedient that we stay sober, vigilant, and prayerful. Jesus instructs us to be ready. As loving disciples of Jesus Christ, we should heed the command to always be ready, while continuing to fight the good fight of faith.

Peter teaches that, "And above all things, have fervent charity (love) among yourselves, for charity (love) shall cover a multitude of sins" (1 Peter 4:8). Because of agape love, we will look beyond men's faults and see all their needs. Solomon teaches: "Hatred stirreth up strife, but love covereth all sin" (Proverbs 10:12). Jesus, who is the epitome of agape love, covered all sins by the shedding of His precious blood. So, let us echo the words of Jesus as He hung on the Cross, "Father, forgive them for they know not what they do" (Luke 23:34a).

PRAYER: Father God, thank You for giving us a warning about the last days. Empower us, by the aid of the Holy Spirit, to be alert, for our enemy goes around like a roaring lion seeking whom he may devour. Let us be mindful of those that need to be snatched from the fire as we see the day approaching. Thank You, Father God, that we have been instructed that Your agape love covers a multitude of sins. Thank You for the forgiveness of our sins as we repent and walk in Your perfect love. I thank You, Father God, that because Jesus loved us before commending His Spirit to You, He forgave us by saying, "Father, forgive them, for they know not what they do". In Jesus' name, I pray. Amen.

THOUGHT: God's agape love washes away all our sins and removes them as far as the west is from the east.

FOUNDATIONAL SCRIPTURE

"So the wall was finished in the twenty and fifth day of the month E'lul,
in fifty and two days."
Nehemiah 6:15

TODAY'S SCRIPTURE

"Let love be without dissimulation. Abhor that which is evil; cleave to
that which is good Be kindly affectioned one to another with brotherly
love; in honor preferring one another."
Romans 12:9-10

EXHORTATION: Today's Scripture should summon us to let love be without dissimulation. The writer is encouraging us to portray true and real love instead of pretend or false love. We may appear to love others, but what is in our hearts will eventually be known, for nothing is hidden that God will not reveal. God knows us better than we know ourselves. Therefore we must ask as King David, for God to search our hearts and reveal its intents. He sees the evil of our hearts, because as a man thinketh in his heart, so is he. We should remember that, "There is a time for everything, a time to love and a time to hate" (Ecclesiastes 3:1a, 8). We love people and we hate that which is evil and brings harm to anyone. Paul says, "Abhor that which is evil; cleave to that which is good" (Romans 12:9b). Every day, let us resolve to walk in agape love.

How can we be kindly affectionate to one another? By esteeming others better than ourselves, we are acting in agape love. It is this part of God that teaches us to love one another or to "be kindly affectionate with brotherly love". My greatest desire is to walk in agape love with others; by loving my neighbors as I love myself. And because God's love has been shed abroad in my heart by the power of His Holy Spirit, I will be able to love without dissimulation as God and Jesus love.

PRAYER: Father God, we want to shine forth Your agape love for all men to see and come to know You as You are. Glorify Yourself through Your love shed abroad in our hearts. God, we know that real love is compassion in action. We will seek to show kindly affection to others. We will esteem others better than ourselves by preferring one another. Thank You, God, for we know that Your agape love requires total forgiveness. So, today, we will walk in agape love by forgiving, forgetting, and moving towards the high calling You have for Your children. In Jesus' name, we are forgiven. Amen.

THOUGHT: Agape love includes kindness and forgiveness.

FOUNDATIONAL SCRIPTURE

"So the wall was finished in the twenty and fifth day of the month E'lul, in fifty and two days."
Nehemiah 6:15

TODAY'S SCRIPTURE

"Owe no man anything, but to love one another; for he that loveth another hath fulfilled the law."

Romans 13:8

EXHORTATION: "How much do I owe Him? How much do I owe Him? He died just for me." This verse from the songwriter's lips, impels us to count the cost of what Jesus paid for our sins. And this little verse of poetry, which I learned in high school, revives my soul whenever I recite it.

What can I give Him, Poor as I am?
If I were a shepherd, I would bring a lamb.
If I were a wise man, I would do my part.
Yet, what can I give Him? I give my heart.

I will give Him the one thing He truly desires, a heart that adores and worships Him alone. He desires I have no other gods before Him. I am a disciple of God and follow His command to walk in His love. Therefore, my desire is to owe no man anything but love. God's Word confirms that because His love is everlasting and abides within us, we must always be willing to share it with all mankind.

Rebuilding the Wall of Agape Love

Why is our love for others called a debt? Because of the lavish love of Christ that has been poured upon us, we shall forever be indebted to love all others. The only debt we should ever owe is love; by showing the same sacrificial love that Christ showed us at Calvary. I will follow the example of Christ, Whose agape love I must imitate. This is an obligation I have been requested to fulfill by my Father in heaven. Jesus said, "Come to me, all ye who are weary, take my yoke upon you, for it is light." The yoke that He refers to here is His love. We struggle when we try to control people with our own love, which falls short. But when we love as He loves, our struggles disappear, as His love transforms hearts and minds and brings light and goodness to any situation we face. We are commissioned to spread His love in a world that is full of pain and burden.

PRAYER: Father God, thank You that Jesus paid it all for me, and it's all to Him I owe. Sin had left a crimson stain, but thanks to God, Jesus washed it white as snow. Thank You, Father God, I am walking in the newness of life, and I am walking in agape love. Praise the Lord! I will owe no man anything except to love him. In Jesus' name, I pray. Amen.

THOUGHT: I owed a debt that only Jesus could pay with His precious blood. I now owe a debt of love in which my Savior calls me to walk.

FOUNDATIONAL SCRIPTURE

*"So the wall was finished in the twenty and fifth day of the month E'lul,
in fifty and two days."*
Nehemiah 6:15

TODAY'S SCRIPTURE

*"And we know that all things work together for good to them that love
God, to them who are the called according to his purpose."*

Romans 8:28

EXHORTATION: I thank God that He called me to walk in agape love. Right now, I stand awestruck, not really knowing the whole of His divine plan for me. But I know that as long as I continue in His Word and walk in His agape love, He is pleased with me. I meditate in His Word day and night. And continue to seek only His will for my life. I never want my life in Him to be lived in vain or for selfish gain. Therefore, I trust Him with all my heart. And I lean not on my own understanding. In all my ways, I acknowledge Him, trusting that He will direct my path. I acknowledge that, "The steps of a good man are directed by the LORD". Therefore, I surrender my will to His will and believe that He will show me His divine plan for my life.

Today, I am a being persecuted and taunted for righteousness' sake, because I seek first God's kingdom and His righteousness through prayer and fasting. I am being accused of unanswered prayers because it seems that I am not living a prosperous life. However, I will pray continuously in the spirit because I know that all things are working together for my good. I will always remember this because I love my Father in heaven wholeheartedly. I know that I have been called according to His purpose

71

and empowered by the Holy Spirit to be an intercessor. I am extremely thankful to my Father that Jesus is an awesome example of being a great intercessor; Who makes intercession for me both day and night. Paul encourages me to "Pray without ceasing" (1 Thessalonians 5:17). I am excited that God's Word tells us that the prayers of the righteous man—availeth much.

PRAYER: Father God, in the name of Jesus, because I am walking in Your agape love, I will not be seized with alarm or fear of what man can do to me. I believe Your Word tells me that since You are for me, none can be against me. When anyone speaks evil of me, help me lovingly respond with kindness. I will seek to do good to those who despitefully use me. For, whatever is meant to bring evil against me, You have meant it for my good. I know You work all things together for my good according to Your mercy and faithfulness towards me. I thank You, that even though I will go through many hurts, disappointments, heartaches, trials, and tribulations, You are my Rock and my Refuge. You are a very present help in time of trouble. In these trying circumstances, You tell me I am more than a conqueror in Christ Jesus. And greater is Christ Who lives in me; than he who is in the world. I am truly grateful, because You have loved me from the foundation of the world. I see Your hand in my life, keeping me as a shepherd keeps his flock. Thank you for proving time and time again, that I am blessed and highly favored in Your sight. In Jesus' name, I pray. Amen.

THOUGHT: Because I love God, I have been called according to His purpose. My Father always works all things pertaining to me— together for my good.

FOUNDATIONAL SCRIPTURE

"So the wall was finished in the twenty and fifth day of the month E'lul, in fifty and two days."
Nehemiah 6:15

TODAY'S SCRIPTURE

"Ye have heard that it hath been said, Thou shalt love thy neighbour, and hate thine enemy. But I say unto you, Love Your enemies, bless them that curse you, do good them that hate you, and pray for them which despitefully use you, and persecute you."
Matthew 5:43-44

EXHORTATION: At times, I feel like Nehemiah. Like Nehemiah I walk in agape love atop the wall, which is what kept Nehemiah upon the wall, refusing to come down. It was his love for the people of God through the power God that caused Nehemiah to refuse to stop the work and come down and deal with the enemy. The enemies in the world that did not know Nehemiah's God, did not like what God was doing through Nehemiah. The same is true for me today. The enemy of my soul does not want me doing the works the Lord has commanded me to do in his territory. In this worldly realm, I know I will face many difficult situations and circumstances that try to block my resolve to obey the voice of Father God and the commandments of Jesus Christ. Although daily I am bombarded with adverse circumstances coming at me from all sides, these fiery trials are thwarted as I keep looking to the author and finisher of my faith, my Savior—Jesus Christ. He keeps me grounded and on track to fulfill the plan God has for my life; which is to rebuild the wall of His agape love.

These trials at times bring extreme testing of my character, as I follow the

Lamb. God's Word tells me that my faith will be tested to prove whether or not my faith in Him is genuine. All who follow the Lamb will be tested through various trials. However, I stay close to the Lord, knowing Him more intimately through His Word; which guides me through these temporary conditions. The more intimate I become with the Lord, the stronger I am to fight the spiritual fight against the enemy of my soul. As I pray and read His Word daily, I begin to receive the ability to discern truth from fiction; while going through trials and tribulations. I am able to see every obstacle hurled at me by Satan (who uses family, friends, and enemies to discourage me), as an opportunity to grow my faith in the Lord; rather than retreat from Him. God works to encourage me through all trials through His Holy Word and prayer. He also touches the hearts of men who exhort me to a greater level of faith in Him; through texts, emails, letters, and phone calls. And all this builds my confidence and faith so I can be assured that nothing will stop me from rebuilding the wall of agape love in fifty-two days.

One songwriter writes in a popular song, "What the world needs now is love, sweet love." I boldly declare that my enemies need me to share God's agape love with them; every time I come into contact with them. I vow, with the help of the Almighty, to keep His command to walk in agape love with all mankind. I will choose to obey the instructions of Matthew 5:43-44 by loving my enemies, blessing those who curse me, doing good to those who hate me, and praying for those who persecute me. When I examine Matthew 5:44, I do not think it is possible for me to love as God has commanded me to love. I begin to ponder that I will not be able to love those who do not love me back, as I try in my own strength to love them. But then I remember, nothing is impossible with the God I serve. And my faith rises, as I begin to ask God to help me love with His unfailing love; which He showed by example from the Cross. I understand by looking at the sacrifice of Jesus, that He came to show a better way to interact with those who would wish me harm. I will love as Jesus Christ loves. I will love my enemies, bless those who curse me, do good to those who hate me, and pray for those who despitefully use and persecute me.

PRAYER: Thank You, Father God, because of Your agape love, and by the aid of the Holy Spirit, I will not love as the world loves—but follow the example of the Lamb. I will obey Your Word by loving all men, including my enemies. I thank You, God, that You enable me to love all mankind as Jesus loves them. Therefore, God, I surrender my love walk to You. In Jesus' name, I pray. Amen.

THOUGHT: We must love our neighbors, ourselves, and our enemies; with the same unconditional love the sacrificial Lamb of God came to show the world.

FOUNDATIONAL SCRIPTURE

"So the wall was finished in the twenty and fifth day of the month E'lul, in fifty and two days."
Nehemiah 6:15

TODAY'S SCRIPTURE

"Love worketh no ill to his neighbor; therefore love is the fulfilling of the law."

Romans 13:10

EXHORTATION: In Chapter 10 of Luke, an expert lawyer stood up to test Jesus with this question: "Master, what shall I do to inherit eternal life" (Luke 10:25b)? Jesus responded, "What is written in the law? How readest thou" (v. 26)? The lawyer answered, "Love thy neighbor as thyself" (v. 27b). Jesus continued, "You are right, do this and you shall live" (v. 28). The answer Jesus gave the lawyer is relevant to my walk as a believer whenever I encounter those I feel are not a part of my circle of people I trust; especially those who I may suspect do not have my best interests at heart. This lawyer is like many of us. We attempt to justify our actions by asking Jesus, "Who is my neighbor" (v. 29b)? I have echoed those sentiments many times. Even today, when the persons I think truly loves me irritates me beyond my breaking point, it causes me to wonder if I can treat them like neighbors as Jesus commands me to do. I become tempted to bring attention to what I perceive as their flaws and misgivings. Also, as I examine my first impressions, I try to justify them with valid reasons as to why I feel that certain people would not make good neighbors. I begin my analysis with the mindset that there are some people who I feel would cause me concern if they were my neighbors. This is when I remind myself of God's unconditional love for me. He reminds me that He gave His only begotten Son (the spotless Lamb) to redeem me and reconcile me back to Him. Once I accept what Jesus has done for me so I can have eternal life, I have no right to judge another as unworthy of the same love from me I was shown by Christ. Therefore, once again I vow to walk in agape love. I look for and welcome every opportunity that God gives me to show His love to a lost and dying world.

PRAYER: Father God, I thank You that You not just told me to love my neighbors, but actually demonstrated how to do so. How can I show any less love to my neighbors and enemies, than You have so graciously shown me? As Jesus hung on the Cross in my place, I have no right to show any favoritism to one person over another. Who are my neighbors? According to Your Word, all of mankind, from every tribe, culture, and nation, from the least to the greatest. Because I have the most wonderful example of love because of You, I can love like You. I will esteem others better than I and, prefer others with honor and love. The love You shed in my heart is not temporary or weak. And because of these facets, it is like no love a man can muster on his own, without You. I thank You that I can love unconditionally with Your agape love. I am determined to walk with love for all mankind; even in the face of adversity and discouragement. I will, therefore, offer no ill will toward anyone. Rather, I will fulfill the law of love by treating others the way that I want everyone to treat me. In Jesus' name, I pray. Amen.

THOUGHT: I thank You, Father God, for giving me the desire to truly love not only my neighbors and myself, but my enemies as well. May Your love in my life bring others into Your kingdom; the same way it did for me.

29

FOUNDATIONAL SCRIPTURE

"So the wall was finished in the twenty and fifth day of the month E'lul,
in fifty and two days."
Nehemiah 6:15

TODAY'S SCRIPTURE

"And the grace of our Lord was exceeding abundant with faith and love
which is in Christ Jesus."
1 Timothy 1:14

EXHORTATION: God's Word admonishes believers to live a life that shows that He lives within us. And how we do this is through the following Scripture: "That Christ dwell in your hearts by faith; that ye, being rooted and grounded in love" (Ephesians 3:17). As outlined in Ephesians 3:20, because I have the grace (God's unmerited favor) of our loving Lord, I am now able through Christ, to do exceeding abundantly above all that I ask or think; according to the power that works in me. This exhortation excites me, because it proves I am part of His eternal Kingdom. Therefore, I boldly proclaim that because of His love I am like a tree that is planted by the waters. I shall not be moved, because the Lord has provided for me to overcome in this world. I will not be moved by the wisdom of men, but only by the wisdom of an omnipotent and omniscient God. I am thankful to God who generously gives me His wisdom when I ask Him for it.

I am grateful God, that You have not given me a spirit of fear, but You have given me power, love and a sound mind. Because God's grace is sufficient for me, I have His grace and mercy to walk in faith and agape love, which is in Christ Jesus. I am elated that Your mercy, O God, and Your goodness shall follow me all the days of my life, as promised in Psalm 23:6a.

PRAYER: Father, because Your grace is sufficient for me, I can walk in faith in Christ Jesus. I am elated that Your mercy and Your goodness shall follow me all the days of my life, as promised in Psalm 23. Father I thank You and praise You for being my El Shaddai, the All-Sufficient One in my life. I am overflowing with Your grace and Your mercy. I thank You that Your mercies are new every morning. God, I want to show Your mercy and Your lovingkindness to all mankind. God, I am entering Your presence with praise and thanksgiving. I humbly bow at Your feet. I am grateful that You have not given me a spirit of fear, but You have given me power, love, and a sound mind. I thank You for Your agape love as demonstrated through Your Son, my redeemer. I vow to live surrendered to Your will; that calls me to love and give myself to You, a living, loving sacrifice. In Jesus' name, I pray. Amen.

THOUGHT: I believe that God will bless and enlarge my territory to spread His agape love.

FOUNDATIONAL SCRIPTURE

"So the wall was finished in the twenty and fifth day of the month E'lul, in fifty and two days."
Nehemiah 6:15

TODAY'S SCRIPTURE

"Seeing ye have purified your souls in obeying the truth through the Spirit unto unfeigned love of the brethren, see that ye love one another with a pure heart fervently."
1 Peter 1:22

EXHORTATION: On the eve of the historic presidential election between Senator Barack Obama and Senator John McCain, I felt an urgency to pray that men and women across the nation, would cast their ballots with sincere and unfeigned love in their hearts. Borrowing from a speech by the late Dr. Martin Luther King, Jr., in 1963 during his historic March on Washington, I prayed the same prayer he prayed; for those who would be voting for new leaders in our nation. I prayed that voters "would not judge [these men] by the color of [their] skin, but by the content of [their] character." God's Word implores believers to pray for those in leadership, because anyone in leadership is ultimately placed there by His power and authority. I will daily pray for all authorized leaders around the globe; that they may find the God of agape love. I will encourage other prayer warriors to do the same. I pray God's will be done in earth as it is in heaven, through the prayers of the saints, as He reaches the hearts of all leaders through His control of circumstances in the earth.

In 1 Peter 1:22, we are instructed to fervently love one another with pure hearts. God, please give me a spirit of love and a passion to love as You love. For You so loved us that You gave Your only begotten Son, Jesus, to shed His precious blood for the remission of our sins. I will extend God's agape love to my brothers and sisters in Christ, my family, my friends, and even my enemies.

PRAYER: Father, because of Your love for the world, I seek Your will for the leaders in our nation and around the world. I trust that You are the Most High God; who knows the hearts of all men. I believe that You work all things for the good of those who love You. Therefore, I will not fear what man does to destroy each other and Your creation. I will rest in You, knowing that You have everything under control. Help me to be sensitive and reliable, when it comes to praying for leaders, whose decisions affect the whole world, and the people You have created. May Your lovingkindness and faithfulness continue in all nations, as I continually pray for the lost and dying who are searching for You. May You turn the hearts of all leaders back to You. Help them find the firm foundation found only in Your agape love for them. In Jesus name. Amen.

THOUGHT: Because the fervent prayer of the righteous avails much, God moves in mighty power on behalf of His children. He wants His children to live in His peace and agape love. Therefore, as believers we must pray without ceasing for good leaders who will follow the Lamb to be placed in the highest offices in the land, so the world will know He is God.

FOUNDATIONAL SCRIPTURE

"So the wall was finished in the twenty and fifth day of the month E'lul,
in fifty and two days."
Nehemiah 6:15

TODAY'S SCRIPTURE

"Fulfill ye my joy, that ye be likeminded, having the same love, be
of one accord, of one mind. Let nothing be done through strife or
vainglory, but in lowliness of mind, let each esteem others
better than themselves."

Philippians 2:2-3

EXHORTATION: On November 4, 2008, I was watching the election returns and concluded that Philippians 2:2-3 should be etched upon every American's heart. I declared that the United States is one nation under God and, that unity among all people would abound and resound with the words: "United we stand, divided we will fall." On that momentous day, my heart was filled with joy, as I prayed we would be like-minded, having the same love, being of one accord, and of one voice. We would be like a well-tuned choir – having one voice and a well-tuned band—echoing the sound of harmony. And the sound we heard was: TO GOD BE THE GLORY! GOD DID IT! GOD DID IT! The first African American president of the United States of America was elected. It had been a long time coming. And by the grace of God, I knew He was doing something no man could take credit for. Praise God, that two cultures would be walking in His agape love; believing that THE BEST IS YET TO COME!

Unfortunately, the years following the election brought a heightened sense of division; that caused a dramatic outcry for God's agape love. There was a climate of dissension between every political leader; causing unrest among the very people who put these leaders in place. There were threats from leaders who did not agree with other leaders; exclaiming that their disagreement could come to the point of wreaking havoc for those who elected them. These leaders did not care that they were gravely affecting the lives of American citizens through causing tremendous fear concerning their livelihoods, mindsets, and core beliefs. Furthermore, even the name of our newly elected leader, President Barack Obama, became a word portrayed with hatred; rather than a name to be honored. And many long-time and powerful legislators were voted out of their long-held seats, because they chose to endorse bills and other proposed legislation that the president endorsed. God's Word says to give honor to whom honor is due. The prestigious office of the presidency is at stake when people of a nation divide themselves; because the one in office is not from their preferred culture. And this is fearful when it happens, because without the office of the president, America would be living under the rule of a dictator.

PRAYER: Father God, I pray that all leaders, no matter their culture, would do all things acceptable to Your glory and honor with lowliness and humbleness of mind. I pray that the president will stay humble in Your sight and seek to give You honor and praise by living a life of faith that is pleasing to You. I pray that his heart is filled with agape love so that he will love You, God, with all his heart, with all his mind, with all his soul, and with all his strength. And that he will love his neighbors and himself. And that he will love and pray for his enemies; as You have commanded. God, I pray for all those who are in authority. I pray that every leader will care about all cultures by showing no favoritism; as they seek Your wisdom and guidance as to how the people should be led according to Your will. May the prayers of Your people bring healing among the leaders, the people, and cause the secular system in which we live—to be at peace and in harmony before You. In Jesus' name, I pray. Amen.

THOUGHT: Prayer changes people. Therefore, we must vow to pray; so God's authority in this earthly realm brings peace, acceptance and harmony among all cultures—without any semblance of favoritism.

FOUNDATIONAL SCRIPTURE

"So the wall was finished in the twenty and fifth day of the month E'lul,
in fifty and two days."
Nehemiah 6:15

TODAY'S SCRIPTURE

"I love the LORD, because he hath heard my voice and my
supplications. Because he hath inclined his ear unto me,
therefore will I call upon him as long as I live."

Psalm 116:1-2

EXHORTATION: I know I desperately need to walk in agape love with all mankind—towards those who are in my life now and those in the future. I come boldly unto the throne of grace asking my heavenly Father to help me love; even when it does not feel or seem natural to me. I must be ready when people randomly show up in my life; with hate and schemes to wreak havoc in my life. I must have God's Word hidden in my heart; so I do not sin against Him. The enemy of my soul works through the lives of individuals who do not know God or His ways. But God's Word declares, that when enemies come into my life like a flood, trying to overwhelm me and steal my faith in Him, He promises to raise up a standard against those enemies. This means I become stronger or more ready for the next trying circumstance that my enemy would try and bring into my life. I cannot avoid the fiery darts that may come against me, but I can be ready through prayer and knowing God's Word, I will overcome. I must draw near to God and seek His will in all these fiery situations; knowing that I should count it all joy when I am tried and overcome. I am encouraged to overcome by the word of my testimony and the blood of the Lamb. Because Jesus died and reconciled me to His Father, I declare and decree in line with God's Word, that there is nothing that can separate me from

His agape love. My Lord prepares a table before me, in the presence of my enemies. And my cup runs over with agape love for all mankind.

I know my Father hears my supplications and petitions. I am thankful that he inclines His ear unto me. And I will call upon Him as long as I live. I will heed His command when He decrees, "Call unto me, and I will answer thee, and shew thee great and mighty things, which thou knowest not" (Jeremiah 33:3). One songwriter wrote these lyrics in an old familiar hymn: "I love the Lord; He heard my cry and, pitied every groan. Long as I live, when troubles rise, I'll hasten unto His throne." I call upon Jesus to make intercession for me and others both day and night.

PRAYER: O loving God, I do not cease to ask You to help me walk in Your ways among all mankind. God, even in the midst of an unfavorable situation, where I am being harassed and unfairly attacked without a cause, I will cry out to You. For You alone have the answers to the cries of my heart. I will love and pray for those who mistreat me and despitefully dishonor me. I will pray as Jesus prayed: "Father, forgive them, for they know not what they do". With lovingkindness, my God, You have drawn me. Therefore, I know when I call, You will answer me and fill me with love, joy, peace, patience, goodness, kindness, faithfulness, gentleness and self-control—for against such there is no law. In Jesus' name, I pray. Amen.

THOUGHT: I cry out to the God of love for He alone is my help. He hears and answers me—showing me great and mighty things that I do not know.

FOUNDATIONAL SCRIPTURE

"So the wall was finished in the twenty and fifth day of the month E'lul,
in fifty and two days."
Nehemiah 6:15

TODAY'S SCRIPTURE

"He hath shewed thee, O man, what is good: and what doth the LORD
require of thee, but to do
justly, and to love mercy, and to walk humbly with God."
Micah 6:8

EXHORTATION: What are four attributes of God that prove His divine love for me? First, I see that He is good. Not a good that man defines as good, but a divine goodness. The psalmist instructs, "O taste and see that the Lord is good" (Psalm 34:8a). And reveals that God's goodness is sweeter than honey. Second, I see His righteousness. Not the righteousness of man, for man's righteousness is as filthy rags. As it is commanded in Matthew 6:33, I will seek first God's kingdom and His righteousness, knowing all His other benefits will be added unto me. God is just and righteous. His Word teaches me His righteous precepts, which will show me His will for my life. I am grateful His Word leads me to live in right standing with Him daily. I am also grateful to our heavenly Father, that I can walk in right relationship with all mankind. And this definitely includes the loving husband He gave me; who chooses to walk according to the righteous ways of the Lord, by walking humbly before his God. I am so thankful that he follows Your command to love me as Christ loves the church. Third, God is merciful and full of compassion. He showed mercy for me when He gave His only begotten Son to die for my sin on the Cross. I choose to be merciful to all mankind, so I can obtain God's mercy. Fourth, Jesus showed me how to walk humbly among mankind. He laid aside His glory and made Himself of no reputation; when He came from heaven to show me THE WAY. I can now be assured that I will spend eternal life with Him in heaven. Finally, I will walk humbly before my God; for He instructs me to humble myself under His mighty hand. And promises that in due time He will exalt me to do wonderful works— that will promote His Kingdom on earth.

PRAYER: Father God, I have tasted Your goodness so many times. You are always good to me, whatever trials in life I face. Your goodness has never failed me or let me down. I will stay close to You and learn Your ways. I will daily seek first Your righteousness. As I stand clothed in Your righteousness, I reflect Your glory in the earth. As I walk according to Your Word, all will see the most significant manifestation of Your glory, Your agape love. I praise and thank You for Your agape love that causes me to have mercy for others. Give me a strong and unfathomable passion for mercy towards others. In order to have this kind of mercy, I must be humble. Lord, humble me by breaking my heart for what breaks Yours. Help me hear the cries of the lost, the hurting, the hungry, the prisoners, etc. Search my heart and show me if there be any wickedness or lack of forgiveness there; so I can repent. I repent and humble myself under Your mighty hand, knowing that in due season, I will be given ever increasing responsibility in Your Kingdom plan for my life on earth. Thank You Father that I am worthy because of the blood of the Lamb, to come into Your presence with praise. I bow down and worship at Your feet. In Jesus' name I pray. Amen.

THOUGHT: Your will that calls believers to manifest Your goodness, righteousness, mercy, and humility; by Christ Who dwells within. These manifestations of Your glory, allow the believer to walk in Godly love towards all others. And it never fails!

FOUNDATIONAL SCRIPTURE

"So the wall was finished in the twenty and fifth day of the month E'lul, in fifty and two days."
Nehemiah 6:15

TODAY'S SCRIPTURE

"Husbands, love your wives, even as Christ also loved the church, and gave himself for it."

Ephesians 5:25

"Then they (older women) can urge the younger women to love their husbands and children."

Titus 2:4 NIV

EXHORTATION: In order to obey the above admonition found in Ephesians 5:25, I ask, "How does Christ love the church"? Christ so loved the church that He laid down His life for it. He became the sacrificial Lamb by shedding His precious blood for the remission of our sins. Ephesians 5:25 is an endowment of a marriage that is based on the love of God. A man should be willing to sacrifice everything for his wife. He should show her agape love always. He should be willing to exhibit agape love by enhancing their love life by demonstrating the fruit of the spirit in every area of their relationship. He should love and care for her as Jesus, the great Shepherd, loves and takes care of His sheep.

In turn, the older women should admonish the younger women to return agape love to their husbands by submitting, obeying, and respecting their authority. Also, they should instruct them to be virtuous women, whose husbands and children rise up and called them blessed; and their husbands praise them. Women in Christ love their husbands and their children with the same agape love that God has for them.

PRAYER: God, I pray that my husband's heart will be filled with Your agape love. Let him have a desire to love me as Christ loves the church. God, let him seek Your wisdom on how he can rebuild the wall of agape love by loving You and by loving his family. I pray that he seeks first Your kingdom and Your righteousness, knowing that You will reward him because he diligently seeks You. God, I thank You for the older women who have trained me to love my husband and my children, through their words, deeds and actions. God, I thank You that Your Spirit of love is guiding me to treat my family the way I want to be treated. I desire to be loved by You and my loved ones. In Jesus' loving name, I pray. Amen.

THOUGHT: Love your family with the same sacrificial love that Christ shows His Church.

FOUNDATIONAL SCRIPTURE

"So the wall was finished in the twenty and fifth day of the month E'lul,
in fifty and two days."
Nehemiah 6:15

TODAY'S SCRIPTURE

"Praise be to God, who has not rejected my prayer or
withheld His love from me!"

Psalm 66:20 NIV

EXHORTATION: As I meditate on the above Scripture, I am praising God for His unfailing love. Because I have the love of God shed abroad in my heart, I know that I can boldly come before His throne and present my request. I pray that UNITY will become the cry throughout the Body of Christ, and spill over into the nations. May leaders, all in authority, and each of us endeavor to put our differences aside and seek God's kingdom and His righteousness, knowing all other things we need will be added unto us. May the agape love of God be the utmost thing desired, as believers walk among those who may come to know You as Lord and Savior.   I boldly beseech the Creator to hear all petitions for peace upon our land. We know He will turn His face towards us and give us His peace. And as we seek to know His will, we believe He will abundantly bless our nation with His goodness and mercy.

I praise God that He have not rejected our prayer, nor withheld His love from us. His Word says that He will never leave us nor forsake us. We are standing in need of prayer. In His Word, God gives us the prescription for the healing of our land. For His Word that will not return void states, "If we, Your people, which are called by Your name, will humble ourselves and pray, and seek Your face and turn from our wicked ways, then You will hear from heaven and forgive our sin and heal our land" (2 Chronicles 7:14).

PRAYER: God, I praise You that Your agape love endures forever. To You be glory, honor and praise for what You are doing to bring Your Kingdom on earth as it is in heaven. God, You exhort Your children to pray for all those in authority. God, I plead the precious blood of Jesus over all leaders and officials who are in earthly authority. God, I thank You for all those You have set in authority; so those who know You can live upon this earth in Your peace. And I thank You that You sent Your Son, Who in His Sermon on the Mount, showed the attitude that all mankind should strive to obtain. God, I am praising You that You have not rejected the prayers of Your children; nor withheld Your love from us. Your Word says that You will never leave us nor forsake us. We are standing in need of Your love and mercy in our lives; so Your glory can be seen upon the earth. In Jesus' name, I pray. Amen.

THOUGHT: My prayer is that God's agape love will bring His children together in unity, as an example to all human authority in the earth.

FOUNDATIONAL SCRIPTURE

"So the wall was finished in the twenty and fifth day of the month E'lul,
in fifty and two days."
Nehemiah 6:15

TODAY'S SCRIPTURE

"And this is love, that we walk after his commandment. This is the
commandment. That, as ye have heard from the beginning,
ye should walk in it."

2 John 1:6

EXHORTATION: I have a grateful heart because God directs my steps; when I lean not on my own understanding, but in all my ways acknowledge Him. I will keep His commandment to walk in agape love; which is a day-by-day, hour-by-hour, minute-by-minute, second-by-second walk; pleasing Him. The steps of a good man are ordered by our loving God. He wants believers to trust Him completely and wholeheartedly; as He shows them in His Word and through prayer; that the purpose of their lives is to reflect Him.

I will walk in agape love, step by step, endeavoring to keep the unity of the faith, through the bond of peace with all other believers. I know that I can walk in agape love, because I have the God of love Who lives within me. I am a joint heir with Christ. I choose to walk in peace, as I imitate the Prince of Peace; Jesus. I will walk showing agape love for any person who comes across my path. Jesus said, "A new command I give you: Love one another. As I have loved you, so you must love one another" (John 13:34).

Rebuilding the Wall of Agape Love

PRAYER: I thank You Father God, that You are guiding my footsteps. Therefore, I am empowered to walk in agape love by the power of the Holy Spirit. I surrender my will to walk in agape love to You. You have instructed me to be still and to know that You are God. And as I come away from the busyness of life and spend time alone with You, I come to understand Your will for my life. Your will is for me to know You through prayer and study of Your Word, which will cause me to act and think like You. And because I am born again into Your Kingdom, I walk by faith and not by sight. And through faith in You, Lord Jesus, I have overcome the world through Your agape love. And through Your great love for me while dying in my place on the Cross, You have given me victory over death, hell, and the grave. And I enter Your gates with thanksgiving and enter Your courts with praise. In Jesus' name, I pray. Amen.

THOUGHT: As I allow the agape love of Christ to rule and reign in my heart, I can walk according to the will of the Father. I will worship at His feet, knowing that as I draw near to Him (and come away from the busyness of life with all its cares), He will draw near to me.

FOUNDATIONAL SCRIPTURE

"So the wall was finished in the twenty and fifth day of the month E'lul,
in fifty and two days."
Nehemiah 6:15

TODAY'S SCRIPTURE

"It is good to praise the LORD and make music to your name, O Most
High, proclaiming your love in the morning and
your faithfulness at night."
Psalm 92:1-2 NIV

EXHORTATION: The Bible tells: "O Lord my God, how EXCELLENT is Your name in all the earth". Your name reverberates as sweet music throughout the earth. I would reword the phrase, "The hills are alive with the sound of music," taken from the movie, "The Sound of Music" to read: "The earth is alive with the loving sound of God's holy name." Because God's holy name, is a name that symbolizes the characteristic of agape love.

I love to call upon the Holy God, Who created the heavens and the earth. I love to worship El Shaddai, for there is no God besides Him. I will tell of His goodness and faithfulness. I will lift His name within the congregation and all nations shall hear and shall praise His holy name. I will proclaim His agape love to all mankind. His love has lifted me to higher heights and taken me where deep calls unto deep. The love of God is rooted and grounded in my heart through His Holy Word. I continue to proclaim, "For God so loved the world that he gave his only begotten Son, that whosoever believe in him, shall not perish but have everlasting life" (John 3:16). I will forever declare His everlasting love in the morning, and His faithfulness at night.

PRAYER: Father God, the psalmist explains, "That weeping may endure for a night, but joy comes in the morning". However, I have joy both day and night; as I continually proclaim Your love in the morning and Your faithfulness at night. Father God, I thank You that because of Your faithfulness, I can walk in Your agape love. Thank You for choosing me to proclaim Your love to the world. Thank You, God, that You so loved the world that You gave Your only begotten Son, that whosoever believes in Him, shall not perish but have everlasting life. THAT'S AGAPE LOVE! In Jesus' name, I pray. Amen.

THOUGHT: I will proclaim God's agape love, which He shows through His faithfulness to me; both day and night.

FOUNDATIONAL SCRIPTURE

*"So the wall was finished in the twenty and fifth day of the month E'lul,
in fifty and two days."*
Nehemiah 6:15

TODAY'S SCRIPTURE

*"Therefore be imitators of God, as beloved children; and walk in love,
just as Christ also loved you and gave Himself up for us, an offering and
a sacrifice to God as a fragrant aroma."*

Ephesians 5:1-2 NASB

EXHORTATION: One songwriter wrote the lyrics, "How sweet it is to
be loved by you." I would like to put my own emphasis on the lyrics by
saying, "How sweet it is to be loved by God the Father and Christ the
Anointed One". Jesus, my Savior and my Lord, humbly submitted His life
on a rugged Cross as a fragrant offering and sacrifice for my sin. I declare
that Jesus is the sweetest name I know. I bow my knee in the presence of
the Almighty, Who chose me from before I was in my mother's womb. I
choose to imitate You through my love walk, by walking in agape love
with all mankind; even those who desire to speak evil of my goodness.

I am overjoyed because I have been chosen to be one of God's beloved
children; by accepting His plan of salvation through Jesus Christ. I choose
to obey the Lord daily, as I surrender my will to Him. I present my body
as a living sacrifice and fragrant offering to Him. I surrender my prayer
life to Him. My utmost prayer is that I will always love others as He loves
me.

PRAYER: Father God, I offer my love walk, and prayer walk to You. I choose to love and pray for those who persecute me. I will pray for those who speak all manner of evil against me. I know it is the ploy of my enemy to steal my faith in You. However, this will never happen, because You will never leave me nor forsake me. You will lead me not into temptation but deliver me from the evil one. Your love will always keep me from evil, for against Your love there is no law. Your love keeps me holy before You, as I live a repentant lifestyle before You. Sin will have no part in my life, as I practice living according to Your righteousness; by the grace You give me. Your grace does not give me a license to sin but takes away my desire to sin and do evil against You. Your grace, when I apply it properly to my life, allows me to walk according to Your ways; the best I can. As I live a life of practicing righteousness and stay in the spirit of intercession, I mature and walk upright before You. Father, I choose to walk in Your agape love at all times, because I love You. I choose You to be my first love. I relinquish my will to Jesus, Who commands me to: Love the Lord my God with all my heart, with all my soul, with all my mind, and with all my strength. And when I love my Savior first, and follow His commands because I love Him, He gives me the desire to love all mankind—as I love myself—and my enemies as well. In Jesus' name, I pray. Amen.

THOUGHT: God, how sweet is Your agape love throughout all the earth.

FOUNDATIONAL SCRIPTURE

"So the wall was finished in the twenty and fifth day of the month E'lul,
in fifty and two days."
Nehemiah 6:15

TODAY'S SCRIPTURE

"Give thanks to the LORD, for he is good, his love endures forever."
1 Chronicles 16:34 NIV

EXHORTATION: "Oh, give thanks to the Lord for He is good and His love endures forever," is a praise song that jubilantly rings in unity from the lips of the congregation. God's people praise Him for His goodness and lovingkindness that He has for mankind. God's grace and mercy were portrayed as Jesus, our substitute, hung on the Cross at Calvary; even while we were sinners. While Jesus shed His precious blood for the remission of our sins, He prayed to the Father and said: "Father, forgive them, for they know not what they do" (Luke 23:34a). Because of His Father's agape love for mankind, Jesus could lovingly surrender by saying: "Father, into thy hand I commend my Spirit" (v. 46) and "It is finished" (John 19:30b). Agape love called upon Jesus to lay down His life for mankind, as a sacrifice for the sins of the world. And because He chose to allow Himself to be lifted up, He now draws all men unto Himself. Jesus is now the good news of the world. In a world full of darkness and sin; Jesus came as Light.

The everlasting agape love now shines through the last Adam, Jesus. There is now a plan of salvation that Jesus bought with His own blood. His precious blood redeems me from the hands of Satan, my enemies, and those that despitefully use me. I am now aware that my Creator, loved me and sent His only begotten Son to die in my place, because of His agape love for me. The Creator made a way through His Son. I am now cleansed by His blood from all unrighteousness. It is awesome to know that my Father in heaven will always love me, for His love endures forever. However, of utmost importance is whether or not I choose to return His love. What an awesome inspiration it is, to know I am loved by my heavenly Father, Who loves me in return!

PRAYER: Father God, I come humbly before You. I surrender my life to You and say to You "not my will, but Your Holy will be done in my life". Because Your love endures forever, I can face tomorrow; knowing that a loving and gracious God will never leave me nor forsake me. Father, I thank You that because You accepted the sacrifice of the spotless Lamb, I am now in the beloved. Your amazing grace is seen by the death of Jesus on the Cross, in my place, as a demonstration of Your agape love for all mankind. Therefore, when a sinner repents, believes, and confesses that God raised Jesus from the dead to pay for his sins, he will be saved. For Jesus' precious blood was shed for the remission of all men's sins. In Jesus' name, I pray. Amen.

THOUGHT: Heaven and earth may pass away, but God's agape love endures forever.

FOUNDATIONAL SCRIPTURE

"So the wall was finished in the twenty and fifth day of the month E'lul,
in fifty and two days."
Nehemiah 6:15

TODAY'S SCRIPTURE

"I will be glad and rejoice in your love, for you saw my affliction and
knew the anguish of my soul."
Psalm 31:7 NIV

EXHORTATION: God's Word tells me that this is that day that He has made. And that I must choose to rejoice and be glad in it. When I think of His goodness and mercy, I rejoice in His unfailing love. I rejoice in it because He saw me in my affliction and knew the anguish of my soul. I choose to walk daily in agape love and the joy of the Lord; which strengthens me all the days of my life.

In 2007, for 40 days, my friend, Henrietta, and I fasted and prayed with a group from Tennessee. The cry of our prayers to God was that He would have mercy on Americans. On the final day of the fast, I praised and thanked God for His love and mercy; which endures forever. In 2008, a new president was elected. How exciting it was when America's first African American president, Barack Obama, was sworn in as its 44th president. Electricity filled the air, as some Americans felt a new hope for the first time in a long time. Americans thought a new day had come that would bring our nation into unity and care for one another. God's people believed that many would begin in humility to serve the living God again. And some Americans believed that God had put a man in office that would follow His wisdom and commands. As a Christian, I was hopeful that the glory of God would once again be seen in our land. The motto rang out: YES, WE CAN! As Christians we hoped that "YES WE CAN"; but in reality, man can do nothing apart from His Creator. So, the prayers of the saints who by faith believed this president would follow the Lamb; found that America was once again led to believe that the answer to the world's problems would come from the wisdom of man, apart from God. However, because some Americans were not led to turn their focus on the Living God, the cry among the believers defaulted back to, we can only "DO ALL THINGS THROUGH CHRIST WHO STRENGTHENS US!"

And because the answers to the problems Americans were facing did not lie with a man, immediately following this momentous election, we began to witness a monumental rise in hateful acts, speeches, and words; not only from the secular world, but from some of the most prominent Christians throughout the nation. I was disappointed, but I resolved that no matter what, I was going to continue to rejoice every day as my God commanded. I knew I could always trust in God's agape love; because it always conquers hatred. I realized that no matter who was elected to the office of the president, it is the heart of one man at a time that Jesus came to change by dying on the Cross. No government will ever be able to legislate righteousness or change the heart of mankind. Only the agape love of God, working by His Holy Spirit, will any person see they need to humble themselves before their Creator. Only the Holy Spirit can lead mankind to understand that they need a Savior. And once mankind is faced with the truth of the good news of Jesus Christ, they alone must make the decision to choose His way or not.

PRAYER: Father God, have mercy on Americans. God, because of Your great love, we can rejoice in Your agape love, because You have seen the affliction and the anguish of Your people. God, because of the love that is shed abroad in our hearts, Your people will walk humbly before You. We will pray and seek Your face. We vow to turn from our wicked ways. Thank You, Father God, Your Word tells us You will hear from heaven, forgive our sin, and heal our land. God, I thank You that, You saw before the foundation of the world, that Americans would need a supernatural healing. God, I thank You that You have ordained powerful, prevailing intercessors for Americans during their troubled times. In Jesus' name, I pray. Amen.

THOUGHT: We rejoice in the agape love You have for all who live in America and the world. We ask and believe that Your Holy Spirit will convict sinners, as we pray for the souls of the lost. And may the leaders in America bow their knees before the King of kings and Lord of lords!

FOUNDATIONAL SCRIPTURE

"So the wall was finished in the twenty and fifth day of the month E'lul, in fifty and two days."
Nehemiah 6:15

TODAY'S SCRIPTURE

"But I will sing of your strength, in the morning I will sing of your love: for you are my fortress, my refuge in times of trouble. You are my strength, I sing praise to you; you, God, are my fortress, my God on whom I can rely."

Psalm 59:16-17 NIV

EXHORTATION: One of my favorite inspirational praise chorus: O God, I love to praise You, I love to praise Your name. O how I love to praise Your holy name. I come today, praising You just because of Who You are. You are my strength and, in the early morning, I sing of Your great love toward me. Today and every day, I can rejoice and sing because You are my fortress and my refuge in times of trouble.

Because the joy of the Lord is my strength, I can praise my loving God. I am so thankful that His great love endures forever. I will praise Him in the morning; I will praise Him in the noon time; I will praise Him when the sun goes down. I will praise the Lord, for He is my Savior, my Lord, my Shepherd, my agape love, my joy, and my peace. God is everything that I need. In Him, I move and have my being. He is the author and the finisher of my faith. I am a believer and not a doubter. Therefore, I constantly remind myself to always have faith in God.

PRAYER: Father God, I thank You that I can lean and depend on Your everlasting and loving arms. With Your strong arms, You will strengthen me where I am weak, and build me up when I am downtrodden. Because of the agape love You show me daily, every morning I can sing of Your greatness in my life. O God, I love to praise You. I love to praise Your name. O how I love to praise Your holy name. I praise You just because of Who You are. You are my strength and high tower. I sing of Your great love toward me. Every day I rejoice and sing, because You are my fortress and my refuge in times of trouble. I boldly declare that I will dwell in the shadow of the Almighty. Thank You for Your love for me. Thank you for forgiving all my sins, when I cry out for Your mercy and forgiveness. Because I have been saved by Your loving grace, I exuberantly shout, "I am redeemed by the blood of the Lamb". In Jesus' name, I pray. Amen.

THOUGHT: I will sing of my God, for He alone is my strength, my fortress, my refuge, and my agape love; all the days of my life.

FOUNDATIONAL SCRIPTURE

"So the wall was finished in the twenty and fifth day of the month E'lul,
in fifty and two days."
Nehemiah 6:15

TODAY'S SCRIPTURE

"The LORD thy God in the midst of thee is mighty, he will save, he will
rejoice over thee with joy; he will rest in his love, he will joy over thee
with singing."

Zephaniah 3:17

EXHORTATION: "We sing praises to Your name, O God, praises to Your name, O Lord, For Your name is great and worthy to be praised." This chorus is a song to worship and to the praise the Almighty God. What a mighty God we serve. My mouth shall always be filled with His praise, as I remain filled with His Holy Spirit. I will bow down and worship Him in spirit and truth. I come into His presence by the blood of the Lamb, to magnify His holy name. O, come magnify the Lord with me, let us exalt His name together.

I am overjoyed to know that Almighty God is in the midst of my praise. It excites me to know that God has commissioned believers to spread the good news of Jesus Christ, by His agape love for all mankind. I am filled with joy to know that my heavenly Father sings over us. A songwriter once penned a revelation of God's reality to him through these gospel song lyrics, "Up above my head, I hear music in the air, and I believe, I say I really do believe, there is a God up there." I know why I sing. I sing and rejoice because I am dwelling in the presence of a loving God, Who showed His agape love to all mankind; while we were yet sinners. And through the agape love shed in our hearts by His Holy Spirit, believers are freed from sin; to walk in agape love.

PRAYER: Father God, I thank You that I am covered with Your agape love through the precious blood of Jesus. I am overjoyed when I think about what You have done for me. You so loved me that You gave Your only begotten Son, Jesus, Who shed His precious blood on the Cross at Calvary. It is no longer I who lives, but Christ Who lives in me. His resurrection power of life in me gives me life more abundant. I thank You that You are just and forgive me when I confess my sins. Therefore, I can live an abundant life free of guilt, shame, and unrighteousness. Father, I ask for Your forgiveness every day; when I realize I have sinned against You or mankind in word or deed. Father, I thank You, that in spite of my unloving actions and because of Your compassion and agape love in action, I can rejoice and be exceedingly glad. I know that as I humble myself, by asking for Your forgiveness and the forgiveness of mankind, great is my reward in heaven. What a reward! The reward that brings me rest in Your love; as I rejoice in the song of deliverance You sing over me. In the blessed name of Jesus, I pray. Amen.

THOUGHT: We must be glad this joyous day, for God takes delight in His people. With His agape love, He calms all our fears. He rejoices over us with singing.

FOUNDATIONAL SCRIPTURE

"So the wall was finished in the twenty and fifth day of the month E'lul,
in fifty and two days."
Nehemiah 6:15

TODAY'S SCRIPTURE

"And we beseech you, brethren, to know them which labour among you,
and are over you in the Lord, and admonish you; And to esteem them
very highly in love for their work's sake.
And be at peace among yourselves."

1 Thessalonians 5:12-13

EXHORTATION: The International Version of today's Scripture instructs us, "Brothers, respect those who work hard among you, who are over you in the Lord and who admonish you. Hold them in the highest regard in love because of their work. Live in peace with others" (1 Thessalonians 5:12-13, NIV). I thank the heavenly Father that He continually blesses those He knows will be a blessing to others. "This is the day that the Lord hath made, let us rejoice and be glad in it" (Psalm 118:24). I believe that God asks believers to honor leaders that He has called to oversee His flock. Therefore, I wish to honor my pastor, Reverend Conway Terrell Jones. I honor him for his tireless care and concern for the spiritual health of one of the local churches within the community. For twelve months, he worked diligently with little or no remuneration. The congregation, through a love offering, happily showed the great esteem we have for our pastor. He has not relented in showing forth the agape love of Christ to all. I encourage every believer to honor their pastors; who are called by God to oversee them. I pray that pastors do not lord over their flock, but serve them with the same servant heart as Jesus served His apostles while on earth. Jesus humbled Himself to show all believers how to treat one another; within the Body of Christ.

Also, Paul encourages believers in Romans 12:18, "If it be possible, as much as it lieth in you, live peaceably with all men". Let the peace of God rules in our hearts and He will give us a peace that passes ALL understanding. For the fruit of the spirit is love, joy, peace, longsuffering, gentleness, goodness, faith, meekness, temperance: against such there is no law (Galatians 5:22-23).

PRAYER: Father God, I thank You that You placed it on a congregant's heart at the church I attend, to ask for a love offering for our pastor. I pray that each person gave cheerfully and lovingly from a heart filled with agape love. I thank You, Lord, that You gave the greatest Gift of all to pay the ransom for the salvation of our pastor. I ask You to watch over Your leaders who are to equip the saints for the work of the ministry. I thank You for the pastors of Your flock. Jesus, I thank You that You paid it all and set gifted persons into the Body of Christ around the world. I praise You for Your unsurpassable wisdom, as the gifted persons You called to serve the Body of Christ take their rightful places. I also pray that You expose those persons who would harm the flock; those who are false teachers and false prophets. I pray that wolves in sheep's clothing, among Your people, be found out and removed from among Your people. In Jesus' name, I pray. Amen.

THOUGHT: I will highly honor my pastor, and all leaders, with agape love.

FOUNDATIONAL SCRIPTURE

"So the wall was finished in the twenty and fifth day of the month E'lul,
in fifty and two days."
Nehemiah 6:15

TODAY'S SCRIPTURE

"Turn to me and have mercy on me, as you always do to those
who love your name."

Psalm 119:132 NIV

EXHORTATION: O Lord, how EXCELLENT is Your name in all the earth. I really love the name of the Lord. For at the name of Jesus, every knee will bow, and every tongue will confess that He is Lord. I revere all Your names that show the various attributes of Your glory and character. You are Jehovah-Jireh, provider; Jehovah-Rapha, healer; and Jehovah-Shalom, peace; and El Rachum, Compassionate God; and El Shaddai, Almighty God. For anything mankind needs at any time, You bear a name for it all. You are all in all. I praise Your wonderful and loving name. Father, because You are the All-Sufficient One, believers can come boldly before Your throne of grace. I will bring my supplications and petitions before my Father with thanksgiving. He is my Father in heaven and withholds no good thing from His children. I love to call upon His holy name. I am thankful for the privilege to be able to praise Him—any time, any place, and anywhere. I am overjoyed because His mercies are new every morning. His compassionate mercy for His sons and daughters endures forever.

You turn Your loving ear to me, when I call on You, Abba Father. I know that when I ask, You will create in me a clean heart; and renew a right spirit within me. Therefore, I come to You with a repentant heart, asking

You to fill my heart with Your agape love. I am grateful that You always hear my humble cry; when I bow before Your throne of grace—with a heart filled with love and thanksgiving.

PRAYER: My prayer is that You open doors and empower me to tell of Your Excellent Name in all the earth. Thank You that because You are All-Sufficient I can totally trust and rely on You as Abba Father. With Your praise on my lips, I shout of Your goodness and mercy among the nations. The nations shall hear and praise Your holy and loving name. Father, I choose to walk in Your agape love with confidence. Also, because of Your lovingkindness, I have favor with You and man. Thank You, God, that in Jesus' name, I am blessed and highly favored. In Jesus' name, I pray. Amen.

THOUGHT: God is love, and His name is EXCELLENT in all the earth.

FOUNDATIONAL SCRIPTURE

"So the wall was finished in the twenty and fifth day of the month E'lul,
in fifty and two days."
Nehemiah 6:15

TODAY'S SCRIPTURE

"Watch ye, stand fast in the faith, quit you like men, be strong.
Let all things be done with charity (love)."
I Corinthians 16:13-14

EXHORTATION: "Not by might, nor by power, but by My Spirit, saith the LORD of hosts" (Zechariah 4:6). After we have done all we can do, we just stand. In Joshua 1:9, God commanded Joshua to be strong and courageous. Also, the Word instructs us to be steadfast, unmovable, always abounding in the work of the Lord, knowing that our labor is not in vain. At this point of the journey, rebuilding the wall by walking in agape love has become laborious. During this phase of the journey, I have wanted to quit. However, I am reminded, that my beloved Abba Father, will never give up on me. And He is continually empowering me to finish this wall; by His grace, His strength, and His mercy working in my life daily.

I take up the yoke of my Savior, Who says that His yoke is light. His yoke is accomplishing all I have to do in His agape love. The kind of love that will never fail, in any situation. I will let everything I do be done with His love, because I am not doing it to be seen by mankind; but in order to please my heavenly Father. It is His favor I seek. I will watch, fight, and pray. I believe and trust in God's agape love for me. Because I choose to do my deeds to please my heavenly Father, I walk by faith and not by sight. I have faith that I will be rescued from any unlovable situations. I believe that my broken heart will be mended because the God of love is near to the brokenhearted. I will continue to walk in agape love with the joy of the Lord as my strength. I will not falter nor stumble, because God is ordering my footsteps to walk in agape love.

PRAYER: Father God, have mercy on me today. I desire to feel Your loving presence. God, please be with me as I walk along life's highway. On this highway, I will walk in agape love with all mankind. I am rebuilding the wall with agape love, and I cannot come down. Thank You, Father God, in the name of Jesus and, by the aid of the Holy Spirit, this wall will be completed in fifty-two days. I have seven days remaining. But for the grace and the agape love of God, I would not have made it this far on my agape love walk. In the name of Jesus, Who is my total trust, the wall is already finished; even before my eyes behold it! Amen.

THOUGHT: Be strong, brave, steadfast, and walk in faith, believing that the wall being built, is the very light and beacon in accordance with the Word of God. This wall is a monument that decrees; that all a believer does, must derive from walking the earth in agape love.

FOUNDATIONAL SCRIPTURE

"So the wall was finished in the twenty and fifth day of the month E'lul,
in fifty and two days."
Nehemiah 6:15

TODAY'S SCRIPTURE

"Nevertheless, I have somewhat against thee (the church at Ephesus)

because thou hast left thy first love."

Revelations 2:4

EXHORTATION: Revelation 2:1-4, expounds on how the church is doing many notable things. He, the Master, instructs John the Revelator to: "Write this to Ephesus, to the Angel of the Church. The one with Seven Stars in his right-fist grip. Striding through the golden seven-light's circle speaks:" (The Message Bible)

"I see what you've done, your hard, hard work and Your refusal to quit. I know you can't stomach evil; that you weed out apostolic pretenders. I know your persistence, your courage in my cause, that you never wear out. But you walked away from your first love—why?"

As believers, we must not involve ourselves with anything that takes the place of our devotions to the One, Who died to save us. We often speak of love at first sight. We say that we love God because He first loved us. When we began our Christian life, we were so in love with God, the Father, and Jesus, His Son. We relaxed in His loving arms, to learn of His ways and live every day close to Him. Then one day, we slipped out of the loving reach of a Father Who loves us so much, that He gave

His only begotten Son to die in our place. We became comfortable in the world again, letting down our shield of faith. We have walked away from God's Word and closeness with Him through prayer, to spend more time becoming friends of the world system and the people who do not serve the living God. We forgot that God wants us to keep our total focus on Him; and no longer be entangled with the cares of this world. We wanted to be men pleasers by doing things for an outward showing; instead of obeying a loving Father, Who commands us to do everything we do to please Him. We have discovered that we say we love God with our lips, but it is apparent that our hearts are proving us wrong.

PRAYER: Father God, forgive me for walking away from my first love. I surrender my will to You, to once again walk closely with You as I study Your Word. I choose to stay in agape love with You and all mankind. God, let each exhortation I do, be done in agape love. Let the love that is shed abroad in my heart, by the Holy Spirit, enable me to love You, Father God, with all my heart, with all my soul, with all my mind, and with all my strength. In the name of Jesus, let me love my neighbors as I love myself. Because of this, all men will know that I am Your disciple because I have love one to another. Let me love You with a pure and sincere heart and seek You first and foremost in every area of my life. In Jesus' name, I pray. Amen.

THOUGHT: My prayerful desire, is to never again walk away from my first love, Jesus.

FOUNDATIONAL SCRIPTURE

"So the wall was finished in the twenty and fifth day of the month E'lul,
in fifty and two days."
Nehemiah 6:15

TODAY'S SCRIPTURE

"But as touching brotherly love ye need not that I write unto you;

for ye yourselves are taught of God to love one another."

I Thessalonians 4:9

EXHORTATION: In my study, I have become familiar with two kinds of love, which man is capable of feeling apart from God. (1) Eros means erotic (romantic) and emotional or feelings-based love, and (2) Phileo means brotherly love, such as love between family members and friends. This love was the only love that mankind had or knew; after Adam and Eve fell in the Garden of Eden. It is incomplete and imperfect, but God's agape love is perfect. And this is the most important love needed to rebuild the wall in 52 days—the God kind of love. It is the only love that can truly satisfy anyone's need for love. It is the only real and everlasting love. The incomplete love of mankind will never keep a marriage together without the agape love of God. People ask couples how they stay together for years and years and it is because they have loved each other beyond the love of mankind. These couples have invited the agape love of God to be part of their relationship. In other words, they are both, more than likely, believers in Christ.

Because phileo love, that Cain should have had for his brother, was incomplete, unreliable, unpredictable and imperfect, Cain was able to hate instead of love. For when mankind disobeyed God and fell into sin, they

117

came to know good and evil; hate and love. And because Cain now had the ability to choose to hate his brother and do evil, he became jealous of the goodness his brother chose to display, which allowed him to slay his brother, Abel. God asked him, "Where is your brother"? Cain responded by saying, "Am I my brother's keeper" (Genesis 4:9)? What Cain was really saying to God, was that he could chose to do evil against his brother if he wanted. He had that power now, and he chose to exercise it rather than be obedient to God. The same question is put to mankind: Am I my brother's keeper? However, only believers in Christ can answer with a resounding "yes". And because I am of the household of faith in Christ, I answer "YES, I am my brother's keeper"!

Paul emphatically explained to the Thessalonians his views concerning brotherly love. It is not necessary to write to you because the almighty and loving God has already taught and commanded that as believers we should have love one to another. Jesus said, "By this shall all men know that you are my disciples, if you love one another." (John 13:35). The popular children's song lyrics, "Jesus loves the little children. All the children of the world. Red, brown, yellow, black and white, they are precious in His sight. Jesus loves the little children of the world," This powerful song should not only be a familiar Vacation Bible School song, but a melody that rings from every believer's voice. Disciples of the Lord should all have agape love for their neighbors and enemies as they love themselves; especially for those of the household of faith.

PRAYER: Father God, teach me how to walk in agape love with all mankind. Enable me to show love and to do good to all men, especially to those who are of the household of faith. God, You command us to have brotherly love one to another. God, create in me a clean heart and right spirit, full of your agape love. I will obey Your will and love my neighbors as I love myself. Father God, in the name of Jesus, because I have been saved by Your grace, help me by the aid of the Holy Spirit, to lead others to Christ; who are in need of Your agape love, grace, mercy, and salvation. In Jesus' name, I pray. Amen.

THOUGHT: Let all who know You Lord, show forth Your agape love to all who cross their paths.

FOUNDATIONAL SCRIPTURE

"So the wall was finished in the twenty and fifth day of the month E'lul,
in fifty and two days."
Nehemiah 6:15

TODAY'S SCRIPTURE

"Who shall separate us from the love of Christ? Shall tribulation, or
distress, or persecution, or famine, or nakedness, or peril, or sword?
Nay, in all these things we are more than conquerors
through him that loved us."
Romans 8:35, 37

EXHORTATION: I remain confident and still before the Lord, as the
wall is almost finished. I have been walking in agape love for 48 days.
I am convinced and determined that I will let nothing separate me from
His precious love for me. During this time of rebuilding, just as Paul, I
have had much tribulation come against me and I have been persecuted
for righteousness sake. The enemy of my soul has tried to place a yoke of
bondage on me again and cause me to become depressed by the fears of
rejection and disappointment. However, I am not moved because I know
how much the Lord cares for me. He tells me to cast all my cares on Him,
for He cares for me. And greater is He Who lives in me than the enemy of
my soul. Nothing shall move me from the call to rebuild the wall, because
I am rooted and grounded in His agape love.

I boldly stand on these words, "Nay, in all these things, I am more than
a conqueror through Christ who loves me" (Romans 8:37). Also, the
rebuilding has intensified, because like Nehemiah, I refuse to come down
from the wall until the work is completed. I am determined to do the great

work my Father has called me to do. The voice of my enemy, who would see me defeated because he is a liar and the father of lies. He tries to steal, kill, and destroy my faith and my joy in the Lord. But I will remember the words of Nehemiah, "The joy of the Lord is my strength". The enemy of my soul and those who follow him, by walking according to the flesh, try to make me think that walking in agape love is an impossible task. I remind all my enemies as I meditate on God's Word that tells me, "With God, all things are possible". So, in Jesus' name, I will not come down.

PRAYER: Father God, thank You for Your resurrection power within me, that makes me more than a conqueror through Christ Who loves me. I am a victor instead of a victim, because I walk in Your agape love. I praise You because Your banner over me is love. And You promised that when the enemy comes in like a flood, You will raise up a standard against him. Because You love me and You are with me, I will not be seized with alarm nor will I fear what man can do to me. Thank You, Father God. You have not given me a spirit of fear, but power, love, and a sound mind. In the name of Jesus, I will continue to walk in agape love. In Jesus' name, I pray. Amen.

THOUGHT: In the midst of any adverse situation, I will still build the wall by walking in Your all-powerful agape love.

FOUNDATIONAL SCRIPTURE

"So the wall was finished in the twenty and fifth day of the month E'lul,
in fifty and two days."
Nehemiah 6:15

TODAY'S SCRIPTURE

"And now, dear lady, I am not writing you a new command but one we
have had from the beginning. I ask that we love one another.
And this love: that we walk in obedience to his commands.
As you have heard from the beginning, his command is
that you walk in love."

2 John 1:5-6 NIV

EXHORTATION: In the Scripture, 2 John 1:5-6, John addresses the lady-elect (the chosen lady) about God's commandment of love. He urges the lady (His Church), to have love one to another. He insists that it is not a new revelation, but a commandment that we should walk forever in God's agape love with all mankind. Jesus, Who is love, commands us to walk in obedience to His commands. It is imperative that we follow Jesus' example of obedience. He was always obedient to the Father, even upon and until His death on the Cross.

In the past, in many situations and circumstances, I have been challenged to walk contrary to God's commandment on agape love. However, because of God's grace and the empowerment of the Holy Spirit within me, I will continue to pray for, and love those, who despitefully persecute me. I will love my enemies just as much as I love God. I will love my neighbors and treat them as I want to be treated. Jesus made it clear about how people will know we are His followers. This is how all men will know that we are disciples of Christ, when we have sincere, sacrificial, and unconditional love for each other. The Holy Spirit of God Who lives within me, empowers me to surrender to God's command to live in His agape love.

PRAYER: Thank You Father, that I have been chosen to rebuild the wall by walking in agape love. God, order my steps in Your Word. Help me to live according to Your instruction, to love all people. John emphasizes that this is not a new commandment; it was given to men from the beginning. Father, I cannot thank You enough for sending the One You were most pleased with; Your only begotten Son, Jesus. Was there anything else You could have done to show how much love You have for mankind? How You must have suffered while Your innocent Son, hung on the filthy, rugged Cross; stained crimson with His precious blood. How proud You must be to have a Son that loves You and Your Creation so much, that He would choose to give His life and trust You to resurrect Him. As one who has come to know You and Your ways, by trusting that You gave Your Son to pay for my sin so I would not have to live eternally in hell, how can I contain the joy I have in You? This joy causes me to press on with the knowledge of how much You love me. And Your love inclines me to work with greater vigor to complete my task. In Jesus' name, I pray. Amen.

THOUGHT: I had a debt I could not pay, You paid a debt You did not owe; by sending Your Son to die for me. This took a love that mankind can only dream about. And only a true disciple of Christ knows it really exists. When I consider Your agape love, what joy fills my soul!

FOUNDATIONAL SCRIPTURE

"So the wall was finished in the twenty and fifth day of the month E'lul, in fifty and two days."
Nehemiah 6:15

TODAY'S SCRIPTURE

"As many as I love, I rebuke and chasten: be zealous therefore, and repent."

Revelation 3:19

EXHORTATION: When I am rebuked and chastened by my heavenly Father, I will be zealous to repent. God chastens those whom He loves, just as an earthly father corrects his children out of love and concern for their safety. Because my heavenly Father loves His Creation, He wants what is best for them. Therefore, He made a way for sinful mankind to be reconciled to Him. He tells whosoever will, to repent and believe on His Son. Mankind has been given a way through the Cross of Christ and His blood shed for the remission of sin; so, mankind can repent and live for Him. The words of Jesus, when He walked the earth, were words of agape love; meant to transform hearts and minds. His words were not written on stone, but on the hearts of mankind. It had to be this way, because God does not want a people to worship Him who only do it for what they can get from Him. He wants a people who choose to love and worship Him, because they sincerely love Him; with a pure heart. He loves all mankind, and wishes that no man would perish, but that all would come to Him for salvation. And Jesus came to convict sinners of their sins and ask them to love and trust His Father. He knows that, if the Word does not convict sinners, we would continue in our sinful ways. He came to show the world that the Father in heaven loves them and wants their love and obedience in return. He asks for obedience only because He knows what is best for His creation.

I have chosen Jesus to be my Savior. I surrender my will to the Father's will. I know His will is that I walk in agape love with all mankind. I repent for the times I have loved only those who seemed to love me. My zealous desire is to draw all men with His love and kindness; just as Jesus did. I am elated because He tells me in His Word, that He gives me the desires of my heart. I desire to have His love perfected in my heart. I desire to obey His Word. During this stage of my journey, I am becoming more and more satisfied and pleased as my Father empowers me to walk in agape love. And I am excited about the progress of the wall as I anticipate its completion. I am almost there! I can see the light!

PRAYER: Father God, as I continue to rebuild the wall by walking in agape love, I thank You for rebuking and chastening me. In Jesus' name, I thank You for Your great love that is leading me to repentance. I repent for the times I have not walked in Your agape love. I repent for the times I have not surrendered to Your will. God, help me to speak the truth in love. Your Word is truth. Let me speak words that edify and elevate. "Let the words of my mouth, and the meditations of my heart be acceptable in Your sight." My meditation will be: "I love You, God, with all my heart, with all my soul, with all my mind, and with all my strength. I will also love my neighbors as I love myself. I will love and pray for my enemies as well." In Jesus' name, I pray. Amen.

THOUGHT: God corrects and chastens those He loves. His love cares what happens to all mankind. He knows mankind better than they know themselves, for He created them. Therefore, He take the time to show them the best way; through His Son, Jesus.

FOUNDATIONAL SCRIPTURE

"So the wall was finished in the twenty and fifth day of the month E'lul,
in fifty and two days."
Nehemiah 6:15

TODAY'S SCRIPTURE

"And they come unto thee as the people cometh, and they sit before thee
as my people, and they hear thy words, but they will not do them:
for with their mouth they shew much love,
but their heart goeth after their covetousness."
Ezekiel 33:31

EXHORTATION: God is calling for people who will honor and obey Him in all their ways. We will not only show love with our mouths, but we will demonstrate agape love from the depth of our hearts, which are filled with God's love that is shed abroad in our hearts. We must remember that God's love working through us, calls believers to show His agape love towards all—for actions speak louder than words. One songwriter wrote the lyrics, "I want to know what love is, I know you can show me." People are drawn to us by our acts of love and kindness. Let us continue to show others the love that was demonstrated by Jesus on the Cross for us.

We will not only be hearers of His Holy Word, but we will be doers of the Word. We will obey His commandments to love one another. We will come unto the Lord our God, and boldly declare our love for Him. We will love the Lord, as He shows us in His Word the meaning of love. Finally, we diligently seek God's kingdom and His righteousness, as we consider how deep, wide, and profound His love is for us.

PRAYER: Father, I come into Your presence with thanksgiving and praise. I thank You that You are empowering me by the aid of the Holy Spirit, not only to show love with my words but with actions. Help me to continue to walk in Your agape love with a loving heart, as Jesus did. I will declare Your goodness to all mankind, because by Your lovingkindness, You are drawing all men unto You. I humbly bow my knees to You, Father God, because in Your presence is love, joy, peace, patience, goodness, kindness, faithfulness, gentleness, and self-control, and there is no law written against these. God, I lovingly submit my will to Your will. In Jesus' name, I pray. Amen.

THOUGHT: The LORD is my Shepherd; I shall not lack. Therefore, I will follow Your purpose for my life—to show Your unsurpassable agape love to all mankind—all the days of my life.

FOUNDATIONAL SCRIPTURE

"So the wall was finished in the twenty and fifth day of the month E'lul, in fifty and two days."
Nehemiah 6:15

TODAY'S SCRIPTURE

"And now, Israel, what doth the LORD thy God require of thee, but to fear the LORD thy God, to walk in all his ways, and to love him, and to serve the LORD thy God with all thy heart and with all thy soul."

Deuteronomy 10:12

EXHORTATION: Today, I am rejoicing and very glad. I have been rebuilding the wall by walking in agape love for the past 51 days. Today, the wall is finished with the agape love of God being shed abroad in my heart. The wall that I was instructed to rebuild, by walking in agape love, was finished in the twenty and fifth day of the month E'lul, in fifty and two days.

During this assignment, I had many opportunities to be unkind to people. And at times, I was not as kind as I should have been. This has been a formidable task and my enemies have been there to test my faith in my Lord. However, because of God's mercy and lovingkindness, I walked in repentance. I kept the faith and have finished this particular race. God has been faithful to forgive me of my sins whenever I needed His forgiveness. I know He has forgiven me whenever I missed the mark of His agape love. From this day forward, I, Sadie Bolton Sawyer, am determined to walk in agape love, which is the utmost characteristic that God requires of me. Also, I will revere the Lord my God, and walk in all His ways. I will love and serve Him with all my heart and with all my soul. I will also always remember the embodiment of God's agape love in this Scripture: "For God so loved the world that he gave his only begotten Son, Jesus, that whosoever believe in him, shall not perish, but have everlasting life" (John 3:16).

PRAYER: Father God, now that I have finished the assignment of rebuilding the wall in 52 days of walking in agape love, I will continue to cover this wall of restoration in the blood of Jesus and prayer. In the name of Jesus and by the aid of the Holy Spirit, let me continue to walk in agape love all the days of my life. God, I vow to love and serve You, as well as my neighbors, with agape love. I will also pray for my enemies and show them Your agape love; because You love them and want them to be reconciled to You. When I am persecuted for righteousness sake, I will pray for those who despitefully use me. With love in my heart, let me always love as You love, unconditionally. For anyone who brings evil against me, I will lovingly pray, "Father, forgive them, for they know not what they do." Jesus declared, "It is finished". Now I can declare, "The wall of agape love is finished". I have completed the task You assigned me, during this season of my life. In Jesus' name, I am waiting for manifestations of Your agape love, pouring out of the Body of Christ: bringing about that which You have called Your bride to be adorned with: unity. As I wait upon You, I will continually give You the glory and praise. I will declare Your wall of agape love is complete. All nations shall hear of it and be glad. All shall hear of Your love far and wide, for love has a name—Jesus. And at the name of Jesus, every knee shall bow: in heaven, in earth and below the earth. To God be the glory for all the things He has done. God did it!!! God did it!!! God did it!!! In Jesus' loving name, I pray. Amen.

THOUGHT: The wall is finished! Therefore, every 52 days, I look forward to a daily dose of Your agape love filling my heart and life with Your goodness; that I might not sin and displease You—my loving and gracious heavenly Father. I am so blessed that I can mature in Your agape love among people who need You (people who are hurting, broken, and led by evil); as You complete the work You started in me. I will declare among the nations that Your agape love holds miraculous restoration and reconciliation, for each and every person who calls upon the name of the Lord. For agape love has a name: Jesus!

God Defines His Agape Love in His Word

Love is patient, love is kind.

It does not boast; it is not proud.

It does not behave rudely,

does not seek its own,

is not easily provoked,

thinks no evil;

does not rejoice in iniquity,

but rejoices in the truth.

Love bears all things,

believes all things,

hopes all things,

endures all things.

Love never fails.

1 Corinthians 13:4-8 (NKJV)

CONTACT INFORMATION

Email: sadiesawyer22@gmail.com

Phone: 318-352-1812

Ordering Link: Amazon.com

Made in the USA
Monee, IL
22 October 2020